Q/A about
Bitcoin

From the blockchain concept to the definition of the LNP/BP suite

David Coen

Copyright © 2019 David Coen

All rights reserved. This book or part of it cannot be reproduced or used in any way without the express written permission of the publisher except for the use of short quotations in reviews.

Author: David Coen
www.davidcoen.it
info@davidcoen.it
PGP Fingerprint: 5351632CBBF23EF29F1815ACD270A7681AE508EA

Illustrations: Marianna Prina

General review by: Giacomo Zucco
Translation and english review by: Bitficus, Nuno Coelho (Blue Wallet) and Raljoseph Ricasata (Edge Wallet)

Disclaimer

This book is a study on Bitcoin technology, not a financial document.
Nothing in this book should be considered a financial advice or a recommendation to invest or buy any good.

First edition, 2019
ISBN 9781697134780

Dedication

To my beloved Brunilda, who supports me and endures even when I bore her with my talk about Bitcoin.

And to my niece Arianna, who I hope can live in a better society than this one. Remember the three liberties while searching for your wealth but, most of all, love.

CONTENTS

Q/A about Bitcoin xi

Foreword xi

Acknowledgments xvii

Part 1 1

Bitcoin: Why? 1

    What is Bitcoin? 2

    Is Bitcoin owned by someone (or some company)? 7

    Who created Bitcoin? 9

    Why was Bitcoin created? 13

Part 2 31

Bitcoin: How? 31

    What is the difference between Bitcoin (capital letter) and bitcoin (lowercase letter)? 32

    Why is there a limit of 21 million bitcoin? 33

    Do i need to buy a whole bitcoin? 35

    How are bitcoins produced? 37

    Who or what are the miners? 38

    How will the miners survive when all the bitcoins will be mined? .. 44

    How do you make a transaction? 49

    How do I store bitcoins? 58

    What is a Bitcoin fork? 59

    How do i recognize the false bitcoins by the true ones? 64

    What is the blockchain? 65

    What are the other possible uses of the Bitcoin blockchain? 71

    What is a Bitcoin node? 81

    What is a light wallet? 84

    What is a hardware wallet? And a paper wallet? 87

    Who sets the value of 1 bitcoin? 90

    Can we change the Bitcoin's economic policy? 92

    The spectre of inequality in Bitcoin 97

The "danger" of Bitcoin deflation 103
Why should I convert my savings into something so volatile? 110
How much does it cost to buy bitcoins? 114
Why shouldn't I keep my bitcoins on an exchange? 116
Why is digital gold better than material gold? 117
What is Lightning Network? 122
What is a Sidechain? 133
Was Bitcoin invented by the American NSA (National Security Agency)? 134
Is it true that criminals use Bitcoin? 136
Has anyone ever stolen bitcoins from the system? 138
What does Bitcoin maximalist mean? 141
The fundamental characteristics of a basic trustless protocol 145
Comparison between TCP/IP and LNP/BP 146
Redefining the monetary unit 153
What is a reorg? 154
What are the main critical points of Bitcoin? 161

Appendix I - Best Practices 171

Appendix II - Business modeling in the Bitcoin Lightning Network Ecosystem, by Federico Spitaleri (satoshis.games) 175

Appendix III – One CPU, one vote. A widespread misconception 185

Appendix IV – How much does it cost to send bitcoins? 187

Glossary 191

About the author 197

Sources and References 199

Q/A about Bitcoin

Foreword

"(...) there are problems with the actual use of digital cash in the near term.(...) One concern I have is that the move to electronic payments will decrease personal privacy by making it easier to log and record transactions.

Dossiers could be built up which would track the spending patterns of each of us.

Already, when I order something over the phone or using my Visa card, to record exactly how I spent and where I spent it. As time goes on, more transactions may be done this way, and the net result could be a great loss of privacy."

— *Hal Finney, Digital Cash & Privacy, 19 Aug 93*

The invention of money is what started the trade between individuals and, since then, has permeated our society.

We cannot do without it, but we can learn to evaluate, independently, which money is good and which is bad, which medium of exchange is functional and which is not.

With the arrival of digital payment systems we have increasingly focused on the functionality of money, on the speed with which it can be used, facilitating transactions and eliminating obstacles to its spread.

However, we have forgotten to evaluate whether the money we are using is a good medium of exchange and we have underestimated the threats to privacy that these new systems entail.

Yet the signs were all there.

The possibility for governments to create value from nothing, printing money completely disconnected from any underlying, be it gold or other precious and scarce material, has now become the standard for some decades. From a medium of exchange in the hands of the individual, money has become over time the exclusive preserve of states and central banks.

The threats to privacy were instead fully manifested at the very moment when the Internet was created: governments could finally carry out the so-called mass surveillance.

To counteract these surveillance systems, which could potentially be used for unethical and anti-democratic purposes, a movement was born composed of individuals who shared a purpose: the creation, through the practical use of cryptography, of systems designed to defend people against potential threats to their freedom.

When the sharing of information via the Internet allowed the advent of electronic payments, further criticalities were added to those already existing. Innovative channels were now available to the Big Brother.

Fortunately someone began, with the proper means of the same new computer systems of payment, to hypothesize another way, a possibility of contrast to the system; in order not to let it get out of the way, so that it does not turn our society into a dystopia.

They worked to make those simple theories into real and valid alternatives.

Today we have a tool that represents the synthesis of this hard work and it is up to us to understand its potential.

"We are faced with the problems of loss of privacy, creeping computerization, massive databases, more centralization," and Chaum offers a different direction to go in, rather than governments and corporations.
The computer can be used to protect people, rather than to control them.
Unlike the world of today, where people are organizations or governments, chaum's approach balances power between individuals and organizations.
Both kinds of groups are protected against fraud and mistreatment by the other.
Naturally, in today's society, with power allocated so disproportionately, such ideas are a threat to large organizations.
Balancing power would mean a net loss of power for them.
So no institution is going to pick up and champion Chaum's ideas.
It's going to be a grass-roots activity, one in which people learn how to do it, and then demand it.(...)
The work we are doing here, broadly speaking, is dedicated to this goal of making Big Brother obsolete.
It's important work.
If things work out well, we may be able to look back and see that it was the most important work we have ever done."

— Hal Finney, Why Remailers I, 15 Nov 92

"I don't believe we shall ever have a good money again before we take the thing out of the hands of government, that is, we can't take them violently out of the hands of government, all we can do is by some sly roundabout way introduce something they can't stop."

— Friedrich Hayek, 1984

* David Chaum is a computer scientist and cryptography expert, creator of the concept of digital cash and of the ecash private electronic money. See chapter *Who created Bitcoin?* for further information.

David Coen
Q/A about Bitcoin
From the blockchain concept to the definition of the LNP/BP suite

How to use this book

The chosen formula is that of the questions/answers, therefore, although some topics are addressed in a linear way, it is not necessary to respect the order of the chapters.

My advice is to proceed to a linear first reading, but if you find yourself faced with an unintelligible text, I suggest you skip the chapter and come back to it when you feel ready.

The words in bold usually indicate an important term on which we will return during the reading. Therefore, if you find seemingly complex terms, do not fear and continue: we will analyze them later.

The dashed boxes indicate a particularly difficult piece of text that may require further reading.

I invite you to report any errors and/or deficiencies, but also suggestions to improve future editions, via Twitter @QAaboutBitcoin and @thedavidcoen.

Acknowledgments

This book was made possible thanks to the contribution of many professionals, from the sector and not. I have never seen in any other area the collaboration I have found in Bitcoin.

In an exclusively alphabetical order I would like to thank:

Alena Vranova (@AlenaSatoshi), for introducing me to *The Little Bitcoin Book* and giving me valuable information for analyzing the company without cash.

Bitficus (@bitficus) for "The Sat" and the english review.

Giacomo Zucco (@giacomozucco), for the general review, the valuable advice, the LNP/BP suite concept and for the magnificent review for the back.

Federico Spitaleri (@ FedericoSpital3), for allowing me to publish his article *Business modeling in the Bitcoin Lightning Network ecosystem*, as an appendix.

Marianna Prina, for the fantastic drawings!

Michael Caras (@thebitcoinrabbi), for his availability and for presenting Bitcoin in a simple way in his book *Bitcoin Money*.

Nuno Coelho (@nvcoelho), for providing feedback and reviewing the text.

Raljoseph Ricasata (@ rjrs2k), for the valuable feedback and the extraordinary back cover review.

Silvia Bossio and Stefania Pezzoli for having previewed the text and provided feedback from the point of view of the bitcoiner and nocoiner reader.

Thanks to those who actively work on the Bitcoin code, on Lightning Network and on the layers of the LNP/BP suite and, in general, to the community that chose the cover of this book, supported me, provided interesting ideas and got me thinking.

Recommended texts

For more information on Bitcoin I recommend reading the following books:

The Bitcoin Standard: The Decentralized Alternative to Central Banking, by Saifedean Ammous.
Fundamental book to understand the economic aspects of Bitcoin and the concept of sound money.

Mastering Bitcoin: Programming the Open Blockchain, by Andreas M. Antonoupoulos.
Complete and technical guide on Bitcoin and its programming.

Bitcoin Money: A Tale of Bitville Discovering Good Money, by Michael Caras.
A book suitable for all ages, useful to understand the basic of Bitcoin and money in general.

The Little Bitcoin Book: Why Bitcoin Matters for Your Freedom, Finances, and Future, by Timi Ajiboye, Luis Buenaventura, Lily Liu, Alexander Lloyd, Alejandro Machado, Jimmy Song, Alena Vranova, Alex Gladstein.
Ideal complement to the text you are about to read. It analyze the dangers of the cashless society and answers further questions not available in this book.

PART 1

Bitcoin: Why?

QUESTION 1

WHAT IS BITCOIN?

In the Bitcoin whitepaper[1], the document explaining the main features of this system, we read:

"Bitcoin: A Peer-to-Peer Electronic Cash System"

"A purely peer-to-peer version of electronic cash would allow online payments to be sent directly from one party to another without going through financial institution(...)"

In a few lines many fundamental concepts are introduced:

- **Electronic money**, which actually means electronic cash here
- **Peer-to-Peer** (P2P)
- **Disintermediation**

We will see what these terms mean in due course.

People approaching Bitcoin for the first time are typically frightened by similar concepts, which may sound overly technical, or consider Bitcoin a speculative tool, a financial bubble, a pyramid scheme, and so on.

Confusion reigns supreme.

So what is Bitcoin?

Bitcoin is essentially a monetary system based on mathematics, whose rules (protocols) have been written, in the phase of creation, on the basis of mathematical constants and are not redefined midway based on political choices, as is the case for legal tender money.

To make a simple parallelism, the basic Bitcoin rules are like those of a card game; we cannot change the rules while playing!

Bitcoin is decentralization and disintermediation

This system does not need intermediaries to manage its transactions. Before Bitcoin all digital transactions, from the wire transfer to payments through PayPal, were made possible thanks to the existence of an intermediary. Take for example Alice and Bob We assume that Alice is a customer and Bob a seller: she wants to send him money via the Internet in exchange for a product or a service.
How can they realize this exchange of value?

If Alice decides to pay Bob by bank transfer, she will go to the web page of her online bank (or use the appropriate app), **she will ask** her bank to make the payment to Bob and **the bank will authorize** the payment if certain conditions are met: above all, obviously, the availability of money in the account and the absence of double spending, that is the attempt to carry out a transaction with the same amount of money twice.

So we have a centralized type system in which two actors (Bob and Alice) turn to a "reliable third party" (the bank) to carry out a transaction which, outside of the digital realm, would instead be direct. With cash, Alice would have given Bob the money in exchange for his goods or services.

Basically, when we make a transaction via the Internet, we simply ask the bank, PayPal or any other payment processor to update its records by removing part of our balance and adding it to that of the recipient.

There is no direct exchange of money between Alice and Bob.

With Bitcoin, for the first time in the history of the Internet it has been possible to remove these third entities or "middle men" from transactions and Alice and Bob have again been allowed to exchange money directly.

We will see in this book how Bitcoin makes this possible, what are the critical points of the previous system that led to the realization of this new system and how the currency that is part of this new system is created.

We will therefore see why we can say with conviction that "**Bitcoin is individual monetary sovereignty**".

Bitcoin is digital scarcity

Before the creation of Bitcoin, the words "scarcity" and "digital" poorly bound, indeed, were essentially an oxymoron.

In addition to the ability to execute transactions without a third party that authorizes them, thanks to Bitcoin the concept of scarcity in the digital realm has been introduced for the first time.

Digital goods traveling in the network (bitcoins) are limited like precious materials (e.g. gold) and cannot be counterfeited. Moreover, they cannot be stopped or seized, because they travel within a decentralized network that has no leaders or single point of failure.

Satoshi Nakamoto, the creator of the Bitcoin Protocol, at a time when the currency of the system had not yet found its price, gave us an idea of the concept of digital scarcity, associating the individual bitcoins with the precious metals:

"As a thought experiment, imagine there was a base metal as scarce as gold but with the following properties:

- *boring grey in colour*
- *not a good conductor of electricity*
- *not particularly strong, but not ductile or easily malleable either*
- *not useful for any practical or ornamental purpose*

and one special, magical property:

- can be transported over a communications channel

If it somehow acquired any value at all for whatever reason, then anyone wanting to transfer wealth over a long distance could buy some, transmit it, and have the recipient sell it. (...)"

But what exactly do we mean by the term digital scarcity?
And why didn't it exist before?

The Internet is a tool that allows us to communicate with other users and/or institutions wherever we are in the world thanks to a free exchange of information: when we want to transmit messages and multimedia content to other users, we simply exchange information packets (data).

Even when governments impose censorship on information, there are systems to circumvent this censorship and communicate directly with anyone with an Internet connection.

What happens when we share data, such as multimedia content, on the Internet?

We answer this question with an example.

Let's assume that Alice wants to send a photo to Bob using a messaging system operating on the Internet (for example WhatsApp or Telegram).

Alice's device divides the photo into many small packets of information that are sent via a communication channel via the Internet using a set of protocols and communication rules called the TCP/IP suite.

Once they have arrived on Bob's device, they are rebuilt to create Alice's picture.

In short, Alice does nothing but copy her picture and send this copy to Bob, a bit like faxing.

Before this communication Alice's photo was unique, because it was taken with her device and stored only there, now there are multiple copies.

Alice's photo is not a scarce commodity because it is infinitely replicable: Alice has not signed over ownership of that file but has only sent her a clone.

Thus, before Bitcoin, the concept of scarcity in the digital world did not exist.

Even when, instead of multimedia contents, you wanted to exchange value, you necessarily had to resort to a reliable third party that "kept the accounts" and that, artificially, created a sort of scarcity of resources (digital money) available to the individual user.

Bitcoin, with its rules and protocols, has introduced another way consisting of:

- **a decentralized system**
- **a scarce digital asset**

Two antithetical characteristics to the previous system which is instead:

- **centralized (controlled by "reliable" third parties)**
- **with infinite commodities and digital assets** (there is no limit to the money that can be printed by central banks, as well as the files that can be created).

QUESTION 2

Is Bitcoin owned by someone (or some company)?

Bitcoin is an open source project; its codes, which contain the rules and the logic of the network, are free to use.

We can analyze the code, actively participate in its modification and in the correction of any bugs, distribute it, copy it and modify it, even realizing our own version of the system, not compatible with the Bitcoin network rules.

Parallels can be made with other well known systems: Bitcoin is open source as Linux and Android operating systems, in contrast to closed proprietary systems such as Microsoft Windows or Apple iOS.

Technically, **Bitcoin is not owned by anyone but by everyone.**

Being an open source project is one of the fundamental features of Bitcoin: you don't need to trust the system or who created it. With a little study or a professional, you can analyze the code and make sure it actually does what it was built for.

The system is reliable precisely because it does not require trust. It can be defined as a trustless system.

I understand that it is difficult to imagine that a system that has gained so much importance and has made its monetary unit take on so much economic value, is both free and in the public domain, but indeed the concept of proprietary software, in the history of computer science, came along much later than free software.

Since the beginning of the development of computers and then of the Internet, the technology has been freely accessible. Indeed, this very freedom has fostered its rapid spread!

Bitcoin is no different.

Developers working directly on it do so in a spirit of collaboration, just like those who, at the dawn of the Internet, worked together to create shared rules and protocols.

So where is the profit?

The system by itself does not allow us to earn, but this does not mean that applications cannot be built on it and that therefore the developers do not receive their legitimate compensation. Anyone, a single individual, a company or even a state, can build on Bitcoin, and can do it voluntarily or on payment, just as those who build on the Web can have their own economic advantage.

Think about pay per view services like Netflix, created thanks to the Internet, free and open source system, or "free" services - you actually pay for their use with your data - like Facebook, whose developers are regularly paid and in some cases even handsomely.

QUESTION 3

WHO CREATED BITCOIN?

Bitcoin was made public in October 31, 2008 through a Whitepaper, a document describing the basic features of the system, sent to the participants of a mailing list dedicated to cryptography, associated with the website metzdowd.com.
The creator of the system is an individual or group of people known by the pseudonym of Satoshi Nakamoto, of which there is no more news since 2010.

For years, the real identity of Satoshi has been debated and even today presumed exposures and bombastic statements by characters who claim to be him without being able to prove it, follow each other.

The truth is that it is not possible to know who Satoshi is and it is not even important: as we have said, Bitcoin is an open source system and works well even without its original creator, just as any Linux distribution works without Linus Torvalds, the creator of this operating system.

Changes to the network can become "official" if the majority of the nodes that are part of the system adopts them (see "*What is a Bitcoin node?*"), through a mechanism called "**Consensus**".

Often one is led to believe that Bitcoin was built overnight, without considering that in reality its history is much longer.

In fact, if we consider Bitcoin as an instrument born in 2008 and started in early 2009, we lend ourselves to those who continue to propagate the bad transparency of the system, born "*out of the thing air*".

Would you believe me if I said that the Bitcoin story begins in the 70s? Don't you?

Well, you have to think again!

Bitcoin is in fact the meeting point of pre-existing technologies: from public key digital signature to the cryptographic hash tree structure, from the concept of decentralized sharing between peers to the Proof of Work (PoW).

In 1977, what was then known as the **public key cryptographic system (RSA)** was devised. This system is based on the existence of two cryptographic keys, technically called "direct key" and "reverse key", which over time have assumed the name of "public key" and "private key".

From the name it can be easily deduced that one of these keys can be made public while the other will be kept private: let's imagine that two friends, Alice and Bob, want to send each other a confidential message using an unsafe channel; perhaps one of them is in a totalitarian state, or, more simply, they need to keep their conversations private. With the RSA system, Alice will be able to encrypt the message with Bob's public key and send it publicly. Bob will be the only one able to read the content of the message because this will be decodable only thanks to his private key, which he jealously guarded.

The concept of public and private key has since been used widely in many areas where it was necessary to resort to cryptography and in Bitcoin too: even if the Bitcoin protocol uses the **Elliptic Curve Digital Signature Algorithm (ECDSA)**, it owes its operation basic to the invention of the RSA. Even WhatsApp uses an end-to-end cryptographic system to ensure the privacy of your messages.

RSA therefore introduces the system of primitive digital signatures which guarantees, in the example above, that Bob is effectively the recipient of the message, since he is the only one to have his private key.

The blockchain idea? It is borrowed from that of **Merkle Tree**, a tree structure that uses cryptographic hashes patented in '79 by Ralph Merkle.

In 1983 David Chaum used the RSA and DSA public key signature schemes to implement the blind signatures, a cryptographic technology that allows to digitally sign a message whose content is hidden before being signed and sent; a system that then he applied to its ecash electronic money, in 1990.

The **Proof of Work** is a consensus mechanism that was developed in 1993 by professors Cynthia Dwork and Moni Naor; designed as an antispam system, it was then used, together with Adam Back's hashcash algorithm, by Hal Finney in 2004 to create the RPoW (Reusable Proofs of Work) and applied in its payment system.

BitTorrent (BT), a **Peer-to-Peer (P2P) protocol** for decentralized files sharing on the Internet, to which Bitcoin is inspired if we look at the sharing mechanism between nodes and censorship resistance, must also be added to this list; if some nodes are forcibly closed, the network is held up by the others scattered on the planet (or above it, see Blockstream Satellite network in the glossary).

However, it was not only these and other not mentioned technological inventions that paved the way for Bitcoin, but also theoretical postulates of an economic, political and sociological nature.

Without The Crypto Anarchist Manifesto by Timothy C. May of 1988, the Cypherpunk Manifesto by Eric Hughes from 1993 and the Austrian economic school, probably today we would not have Bitcoin and a digital cash system alternative to the cashless society.

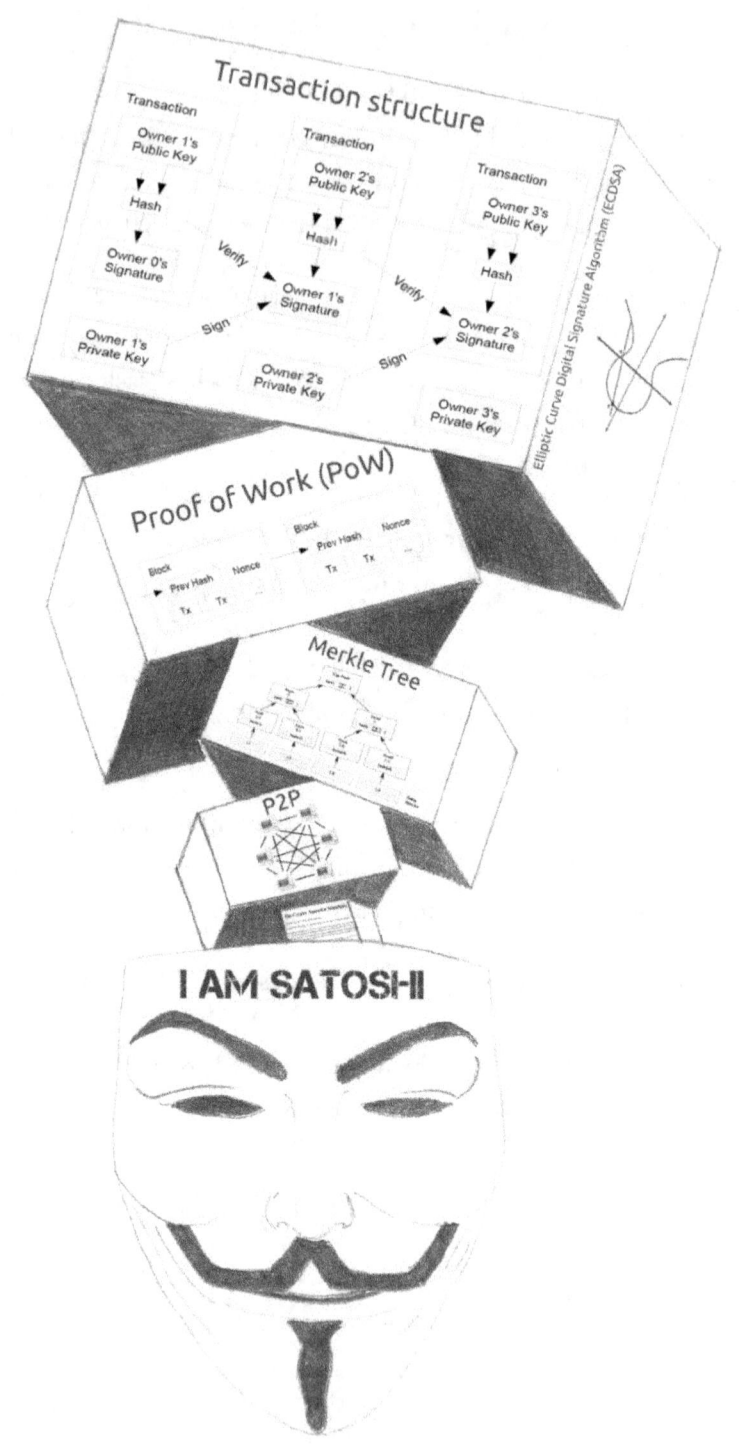

QUESTION 4

WHY WAS BITCOIN CREATED?

Bitcoin was created above all to bring into the digital world what happens in the material world: **the possibility of exchanging value directly without resorting to a trusted intermediary.**

The second reason, expressed in the whitepaper, is to generate totally **irreversible transactions,** avoiding fraud against those who accept payment in cash in exchange for goods/services, without resorting to a reliable intermediary, which is not possible with previous technologies.
In reality, Bitcoin was also created for other reasons, which we will try to analyze here.

The current monetary system has serious problems, some potential, others tremendously current, especially if we consider the digital value exchanges of the so-called cashless society.

I usually divide these criticalities into three macro-categories or types:

- **technical issues**
- **political issues**
- **economic issues**

In this table I have collected the main features of the fiat cash system, ie legal tender currencies in the form of cash, cashless currencies, digital legal tender currencies, and Bitcoin.

Let us analyze these characteristics and the critical points linked to them.

Main Features	CASH Paper/metal	CASHLESS Digital fiat (euro, dollar, etc.)	BITCOIN Electronic Cash
DECENTRALIZED PAYMENTS	P2P payments	Completely centralized payments	Decentralized payments broadcasted via blockchain P2P via Lightning Network
FAST PAYMENTS	Fast near payments slow distant payments	It can have instant payments International payments can be slow	Onchain payments can be slow, LN payments are almost instant
IRREVERSIBLE TRANSACTIONS	Transactions are irreversible	Transactions are reversible	Transactions can be considered irreversible after few confirmations
CENSORABLE TRANSACTIONS	Transactions are not censorable	Transactions can be censored in advance	Transactions are not censorable
SEIZABLE MONEY	Cash can be physically seizable	Digital money can be seizable	Exposed private keys can be physically seizable bitcoins can't
SURVEILLANCE vs PRIVACY	Doesn't help surveillance by corporations and States	Corporations and States can use money channels as a surveillance systems	Doesn't help surveillance by corporations and States
ACCESS TO MONEY	In a cash-only society no one can prevent access to money	In a cashless society access to money can be prevented and prohibited	In Bitcoin no one can prevent access to money
FUNGIBILITY	High fungibility unless marked bills	Low fungibility	High fungibility on second layers
MONEY MINTING	Unlimited by printing	Unlimited out of the thin air	Capped supply made through PoW
MONEY LAUNDRY/ TAX EVASION	Can be fought through the judicial system not easy through monetary system	Can be fought through the monetary system too	Can be fought through the judicial system. Blockchain transactions can be tracked
SOCIETY MODEL	Consumption based society	Consumption based society	Savings based society

Let's start with the technical aspect. Although of crucial importance, it is barely taken into consideration, especially by the press or by those who "are not in the sector", who is not interested in Bitcoin for the moment and/or have not had the opportunity to study the network's protocols.

We have already described the current digital payment system: we have a centralized type system in which two actors (in our example Bob and Alice) turn to a "reliable third party" (the bank) to make a transaction that, with cash, would instead be direct (Alice pays Bob. Done).

Where are the technical issues?

The system described above is centralized: an attacker, such as a hacker, could hack the bank's server and take possession of Bob's money sent by Alice diverting the transaction to another recipient. He could also appropriate the money of both, changing the bank register.

Science fiction? Not really, perhaps a little paranoia. But analyzing the potential threats to the system is a necessity proper to those who create those systems (developers and systems engineers) and those who study and disseminate them.

We should not think of the centralized system as exposed only to external attacks: internal threats should also be considered. These are not necessarily voluntary attacks on the network, but can be technical problems of a more serious nature.

On June 1, 2018, Visa suffered a heavy interruption of the service[2] which caused the impossibility to execute transactions on the circuit in the UK and in the rest of Europe.

Millions of users were prevented from making payments for several hours: an important damage, especially if we consider that individuals also use electronic payment systems to purchase basic necessities.
Real panic arose, which even forced some governments to issue reassurance notices to citizens.

"Don't worry! If you can't pay, you haven't suffered any theft or hacking" The Spanish Guardia Civil reported on Twitter.

> Guardia Civil
> @guardiacivil
>
> Tranquil@, si no puedes pagar no has sufrido ningún robo ni hackeo
>
> #Visa sufre una caída en Europa que impide procesar pagos con sus tarjetas adslzone.net/2018/06/01/vis...
>
> 6:09 PM · 1 giu 2018 · Twitter for Android

Ironically, it was discovered that users could not make transactions through the Visa circuit but were still able to withdraw cash from the ATMs.[3]

A week later, the "rival" Mastercard system suffered a similar crash.[4] Two months earlier, Mastercard recorded downtime in the United States.[5]

As rightly noted by the economic journalist Brett Scott in the article published by The Guardian entitled *"The cashless society is a con – and big finance is behind it"*[6]

"Digital systems may be "convenient", but they often come with central points of failure. Cash, on the other hand, does not crash."

Indeed, the concept applies to both banknotes and Bitcoin, a digital cash system.

Think of it. In its ten-year history, Bitcoin records an uptime of 99.985%: the only two events that caused a temporary interruption of service (in 2010 and 2013), occurred at times when the network was in its infancy and the number of nodes that supported it were very limited, demonstrating that networks tending to centralization (or centralized, such as "classic" systems) are more subject to systemic crashes..

Today, more than 9,000 nodes (according to Luke Dashjr there are actually more than 60,000 nodes!) actively supporting the network and there are more than 10 different implementations of the software running on these machines; this drastically reduces the risk of a system collapse.

However, the probability that this will happen for a centralized system such as Visa is still considerable.

So we have a classic digital payment system that is highly reliable in terms of practicality and, in some cases, speed, but is potentially attackable and subject to technical downtime due to the intrinsic centralization of the system.

These systemic attacks or crashes could lead to devastating damage.

Critical issues of a political nature

These critical issues are usually the most addressed, because politics is passion but also, too often, the imposition of one's will on others.

The example described above is useful, but this time we modify it a little.

Alice wants to send money to Bob, a friend of her, and she uses the reliable third party; the transaction is not authorized. The bank believes this movement of money is suspect so it intervenes in advance to prevent money laundering or tax evasion.

"*Very good!*" someone will say. It turns out, however, that Alice and Bob have done nothing wrong, and that the transactions sent by Alice to Bob take place without the latter providing off-the-books goods or services to her friend.

Let's see a second example.

Alice wants to send money to Bob, in exchange for a certain product, and resorts to the reliable third party. Also this time the transaction is not authorized.

The reason?

The bank considers the good offered by Bob "not positive" for Alice and acts to prevent the purchase, stating that it wants to "protect" its customers. The reliable third party has acted preventively on transactions of private citizens who do not carry out any type of tax offense.

These are not examples in the air and certainly do not represent a serious case of paranoia.

Here a recent example:

This person wanted to buy cryptocurrencies on CashApp and Coinbase using his debit card provided by Well Fargo, one of the four big US banks. The transaction was rejected because:

"Well Fargo does not allow transactions involving cryptocurrencies."

You understand that this is a political choice that limits individual freedoms.*

At this point there are those who say: "*We want to protect the customer from potential scams and highly speculative investments.*" To which I reply: "*Are we users capable of judgment? Why do we need protection?*".

Some realities see this centralization of the system as a way to strengthen competition in financial services but also to tackle money laundering and tax evasion. In this sense, banks, refusing to authorize transactions related to the "crypto world", would avoid being facilitators in case of crimes involving transactions through Bitcoin or other cryptocurrencies.[7]

Others claim that digital payments protect consumers from being robbed or losing money. [8]

In the example above, the problem could be solved by changes to the internal policy or, more radically, by changing banks.

What if "the attacker", is the state?

Wikileaks is an international non-profit organization, known for its activism in the field of clear-text sharing, through its website, of classified documents. Over the years, this organization has spread many confidential documents, including some containing information on the management of the Guantànamo prison camp, which caused a scandal given the repeated violations of the Geneva Conventions perpetrated within the detention facility.

In 2011, following the publication by Wikileaks of confidential documents concerning the war in Afghanistan, the main payment processors, through which the organization collected donations, decided to freeze access to funds and prevent future donations through them.

Among the many providers, Paypal, under growing pressure primarily from the United States, alleged that "[Paypal] cannot be used for activities that encourage, promote, facilitate or instruct others to engage in illegal activities".[9]

Following these unilateral initiatives, Wikileaks decided to accept donations through Bitcoin and communicated it through a tweet.

On this address it received more than 4,000 bitcoins.

WikiLeaks ✓
@wikileaks

WikiLeaks now accepts anonymous Bitcoin donations on 1HB5XMLmzFVj8ALj6mfBsbifRoD4miY36v

1:12 AM · Jun 15, 2011 · Twitter Web Client

Money Control and State of Surveillance

A centralized monetary system implies the potential realization of the Surveillance State, the main characteristic of totalitarian regimes.

A form of cash, better if **sound money**, such as gold or bitcoin, is a tool that guarantees the privacy of the individual who uses it; privacy is fundamental, especially if you live in authoritarian regimes or in countries that, to deal with a financial crisis, actively intervene on the citizens' wealth through measures called "**Capital control**", limiting their free initiative.

In 2009, the world crisis that began the previous year in the United States, struck down strongly on the European Community and Greece paid the price more than many other countries.

According to the former prime minister George Papandreou, previous governments falsified budgets to allow Greece to enter the Euro. In 2015, perhaps the most serious year for the Greek economy, the credit institutions were closed by order of the government and, at their reopening, cash withdrawals were limited to 60 euros a day in order to avoid the total collapse of the banking system.[10]

At the beginning of September 2019 the Central Bank of Argentina announced further checks on money in an attempt to tame speculation and stem a steadily growing debt spiral. Citizens who purchase foreign currencies are required to take an oath: they declare to wait at least five days before buying bonds using the newly purchased foreign currencies.

The reason is soon said: it was customary to buy bonds with dollar and then sell them in pesos and get a profit of around 5%.

This measure follows the limit of money in foreign currency that each individual can buy, amounting to 10,000 USD per month.[11]

In addition to capital control and therefore to direct money control measures, the State can also activate surveillance systems on the population by exploiting the intrinsic characteristics of centralized digital payment instruments.

In Hong Kong, the summer of 2019, a political protest was held several times in contrast with the Chinese influence on the governance of the special administrative region.

This time the casus belli related to an amendment to the extradition law which, if approved by the Parliament, would actually have allowed China to carry out the trials of crimes committed in Hong Kong.[12]
Common Law, a legal system different from that in China, is in force in Hong Kong.
The protest therefore wanted to prevent part of the judicial power from being transferred to another State, with another legal system.
Hong Kong was one of the first countries in the world to introduce a cashless payment system: in 1997 the Octopus card by Octopus Holding was launched, a solution that avoided the use of cash for the purchase of tickets for public transport, including MTR (Mass Transit Railway Corporation). Octopus cards are now actively used also for different purchases, in grocery stores, car parks and other places but also for safe access to homes, schools and offices.
The MTR is the majority shareholder of Octopus Holding.

Guess who owns over 75% of the Mass Transit Railway Corporation?

Exactly, the Hong Kong government.
The government is the majority shareholder of Octopus Holding, which manages the Octopus card and therefore collects data on the transport, consumption and security of citizens' private homes.[13]

Why this preamble?

Citizens, fearing that their card data could be traced and used as evidence of their participation in the protests, started buying disposable tickets for public transport instead of using their Octopus card. This fear is more than justified by a precedent: the police had used similar tracking techniques during the 2014 protests organized by the pro-democracy movement called Umbrella and had exploited them in court against the main protest leaders.[14] [15]

You will understand how a centralized financial instrument lends itself well to state control over citizens' political activities, especially if this turns out to be a non-democratic regime.

According to a recent study by the Human Rights Foundation (HRF), the world currently has just over 100 democracies that govern over 47% of the world's population; 40 authoritarian regimes that govern 1.2 billion people and 53 full-fledged dictatorships that oppress 2.8 billion people or 30% of the world's countries.[16]

Let us return to considering the activity of the third party, in this case the State, on monetary policy and we arrive at economic issues.

Economic issues

The first thing we need to analyze is the potential, indeed, almost certain, lack of fungibility in an exclusively digital monetary system.

We have said that the third party can also intervene preventively and block transactions between two individuals (peer-to-peer) or between an individual and a private company (peer-to-business). Not only that, it can also reverse a transaction and possibly seize the money. This is apparently good and right if this money comes from an activity such as drug or human trafficking.
But what if this money came into the hands of people who have nothing to do with these crimes?

They could be deprived of money considered "dirty".

The reversibility of transactions is a novelty introduced by cashless systems, not present in exchanges of direct value between individuals.
With reversibility, one of the fundamental properties of money is lost: fungibility.

This term indicates an asset that can be exchanged for another of equal attributed value. For example, we can exchange one euro coin for another, or we can exchange it for 100 euro cents; we can also exchange one gold nugget for another that has the same chemical/physical characteristics.
In the digital realm it is difficult to guarantee fungibility in a context in which a third party can intervene and cancel transactions or seize money.

My money could be dirty and therefore not as good as yours.

Bitcoin tries to solve this problem by introducing the concept of irreversibility of transactions and excluding the third party. We will see later that this is not entirely sufficient to guarantee the fungibility of the system due to the traceability guaranteed by the blockchain.

Another economic problem is actually also political: it is in fact the economic policy of the current system.

Until 1971, the global economic policy, already linked to the Dollar, was essentially based on the **Gold Standard**.
The banknotes represented a certain amount of gold preserved in the Federal Reserve vaults and were convertible: you could go to the bank with your own banknotes and get a certain amount of gold represented by them.

In the history of the Dollar, but also of the German Mark and other state currencies, we have repeatedly intervened on this convertibility, especially in times of war, in which more cash was needed to finance war activities, but it was only after 1971, following a series of economic measures called Nixon Shock, from the name of the president of the United States then in office, that we definitively abandoned the Gold Standard and therefore the convertibility.

Since then, individual banknotes no longer represent a reserve of value but are legally imposed and produced "*out of the thin air*", without an underlying asset.

With Bitcoin it was decided to adopt a completely different economic policy from that of the current system, similar instead to that of the Gold Standard because it is also based on scarcity, even if digital.

In the chapter on Bitcoin's economic policy (*Can we change Bitcoin's economic policy?*) we will see in more detail what it entails.

For now it is enough to understand this: the current system does not provide a limit to the production of money and is therefore based on an inflationary model (the more money is produced, the less value the single unit has, the more prices increase), while Bitcoin adopts a limited supply system with controlled inflation.

Furthermore it must be said that the monetary policy of the State or other centralized entities, such as corporations, finds ample room for maneuver within a cashless society. In fact, the presence of physical money implies a tendency to save and to consume "convenient" goods, while digital money encourages spending.

A small side note that has more to do with marketing than with the content of this book: did you know that one of the few advertising investments on paper, still profitable for companies, are the advertising leaflets containing the discounts of large supermarkets?

Returning to the monetary policy of the State; in a cashless society individuals could no longer withdraw, of course, and would delegate to the governments and central banks the entire monetary policy of the system. The example of what happened in Greece in 2015 is in this case a clear preview.

During economic recessions, governments try to stimulate the economy by lowering interest rates, as people are likely to accumulate money to meet basic needs when a full emergency occurs. More money is produced and the one already in circulation therefore loses its value.

This happens not only during recessions, but also in a geopolitical context in which countries fight trade wars.

When, for example, the US Federal Reserve cuts rates to encourage exports, after the same has been done by China, the European Central Bank follows. A perennial inflationary spiral, in which the purpose of the single state is to have the money that is worth less, so that the other states acquire from them the greatest possible number of goods.

Due to the cashless society, individuals' savings could actually be discouraged thanks to the introduction of so-called negative interest rates.

People would pay the banks to keep their deposits instead of earning interest from them. Loans on the part of the banks and greater investments by the companies would thus be stimulated; they would push individuals to spend rather than save.

It may seem like laudable initiatives in the short term, but in the end the transformation of the individual from a protagonist of the monetary system to a pure passive consumer would be completed.[17]

To sum up, on the one hand we have a monetary system that tends to the realization of the so-called cashless society, that is a society without cash in which the value between individuals is exchanged exclusively through financial intermediaries with all the issues that ensue, on the other we have a system, called Bitcoin, in which individuals exchange value directly with each other, created to drastically reduce the technical-political-economic issues of the previous system and achieve the separation of money from the State, as in the past separation from the Church has been achieved in democratic regimes based on the rule of law.

It is often complex to distinguish what is "cash" from what is not.
We are led to believe that cash means "physical", "paper" and that cashless society means "digital", but this is not the case.
We must ask ourselves a fundamental question:
Can I freely dispose of my money?

If the answer is affirmative, then we are dealing with cash: banknotes, gold and bitcoins in our direct possession are examples. It may be material or digital, it doesn't matter. **If I can dispose of the money directly, without resorting to a third party, then I have cash, a liquid asset.**

If, on the other hand, the answer is negative then it is very likely that we are living within a cashless society, or are about to enter it.
Money is no longer cash, but a sort of digital note or negotiable instrument provided by the third party (bank, payment processor, etc.).

It is convenient at this point to take up the comparison table between cash, cashless society and Bitcoin to realize again what this means.

"Bitcoin is an edge against monetary and fiscal irresponsibility from central banks and governments globally."

— Travis Kling on CNN, September 13, 2019

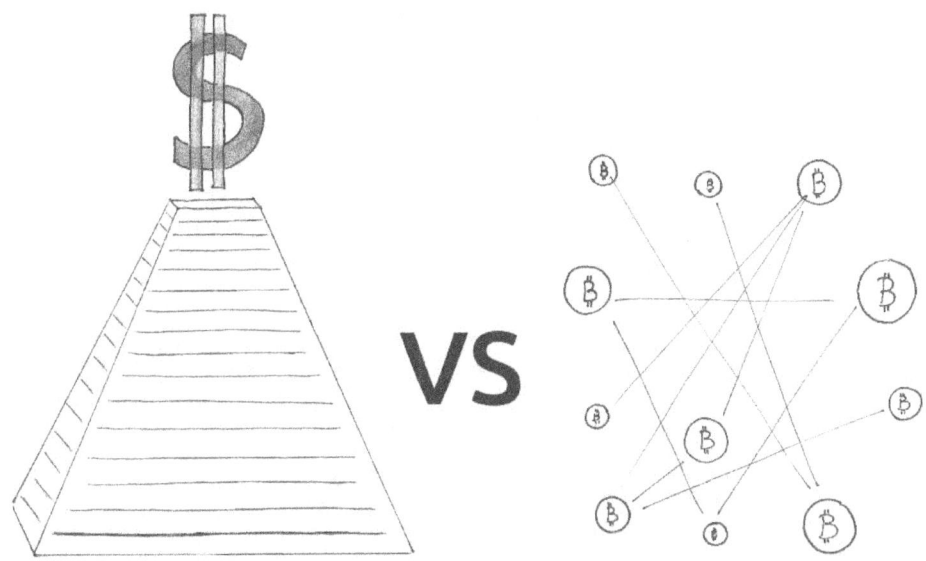

* Note, for the record, that, after the protest by the users, Well Fargo seems to have decided to allow the purchase of bitcoins and other cryptocurrencies through debit cards, while maintaining the ban on the use of credit cards.

PART 2

Bitcoin: How?

QUESTION 5

WHAT IS THE DIFFERENCE BETWEEN BITCOIN (CAPITAL LETTER) AND BITCOIN (LOWERCASE LETTER)?

We have said that Bitcoin is a whole new monetary system but it is also possible to indicate with this name the digital "currency" that runs within this system.

The term **Bitcoin** usually refers to the entire system, including the code and the protocols, while the term **bitcoin**, with the lowercase b, means the actual coin that runs inside it.

We will see later how in reality those who participate in this monetary system do not exchange files (or tokens) called bitcoins, and that therefore there is no currency in the classic sense of the term, but for the moment we take this simplification for good.

We must learn immediately to distinguish these two terms.

In fact we may want to talk about technology without talking about the monetary asset or vice versa, depending on the context.

In order to distinguish these two terms, lately we are trying to name the system "**Bitcoin Protocol**" or BP, while as regards the currency, we are trying to push for the adoption of the term "**satoshi**", the basic monetary unit that has earned its name only following the disappearance of the Bitcoin project creator, or alternatively we can use the term **BTC**, which represents a whole bitcoin.

QUESTION 6

WHY IS THERE A LIMIT OF 21 MILLION BITCOIN?

As mentioned earlier, when Satoshi created Bitcoin, in addition to the decentralization of the system itself, it also defined its economic policy.

Perhaps Satoshi was a black jack player and believed the system win on the dealer if it did not exceed 21 and therefore chose this symbolic number; we'll probably never know.

The fact is that he decided to impose a maximum number of bitcoins that could be created and "cuts in production", called halving, to act on inflation: every 4 years the amount of new bitcoins put into circulation halved and the "production" of new units will end when 21 million are reached, so inflation will gradually decrease until it becomes deflation after the last unit is undermined.

It is often said that bitcoin - did you notice the small letter? - it is a rare asset, because there will only be 21 million units.

In reality, this is not the case.

We can define it as a **"scarce asset"** since a limit to its inflation, to the amount of "coins" that can be "minted", has been established within the protocol, but it is certainly not uncommon or rare. Bitcoin can be defined as a "scarce asset", because it has precisely one of the characteristics that make a good gain value: **scarcity**.

The famous 21 million bitcoins, which are not 21 anyway - approximating by excess will be 20999949.9769 in 2140[18] - are only a useful convention to understand this limitation, in a jargon called total supply.

QUESTION 7

DO I NEED TO BUY A WHOLE BITCOIN?

The bitcoin asset is divisible.

It can have up to eight decimal places!

If we think about euro, we see that 1 euro is divisible up to two decimal places (even if in finance they use more), in this way: 1.00 euro.

In everyday life we also use cents and we know that 100 cents make a whole euro.

For bitcoins things work in a similar way but with eight decimal places.

1 bitcoin can be represented as follows: 1.00000000. It can be deduced that the smallest part of bitcoin is this: 0.00000001 bitcoin.

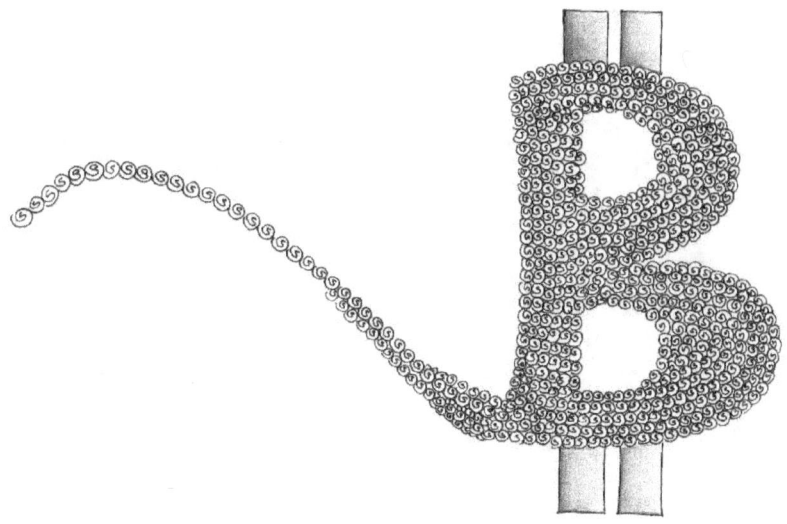

This basic unit, as mentioned above, is named after the Bitcoin creator and is referred to as satoshi.

It takes exactly 100 million satoshis to form a whole bitcoin.

It follows that we could accept and/or buy all the satoshis we want, without needing to buy a whole bitcoin, knowing that more than $20999949.9769 \times 10^8$ will not be put into circulation. For those who are not accustomed to thinking in terms of power, this is around 21 million multiplied by another 100 million units that can actually be spent.

An apparently disproportionate quantity but undoubtedly more suited to a global monetary system, with > 7 billion potential users.

QUESTION 8

HOW ARE BITCOINS PRODUCED?

We have said that there will be a maximum of around 21 million bitcoins (or 21 million per hundred million satoshis) in circulation. But how are these bitcoins "produced"?

We are often led to believe that bitcoins are generated from nothing thanks to a computer, and that anyone can create them with extreme ease.

This idea is typically spread by Bitcoin technology detractors, out of ignorance or resentment towards an alternative and competing monetary system compared to the current one.

Bitcoin undermines the role of the Dollar as the main medium of global exchange and it is therefore understandable that those with interests in maintaining the status quo spread these falsehoods.

Bitcoins are not generated from nothing but assigned by the software running on the system nodes (see the chapter "*What is a Bitcoin node?*").

This software put new bitcoins in circulation on average every 10 minutes, ie every transaction block found.

I realize that this sentence is complex so let's try to clarify the concept of transactions and blocks before arriving at the generation of new bitcoins.

Those who participate in the Bitcoin network can send transactions to each other: Alice can send Bob any amount of bitcoins in her possession. Alice's transaction to Bob is propagated, starting from the Alice node to all the nodes of the network, and temporarily stored inside them in what is called Mempool, a temporary memory.
Each node of the network has its own Mempool.

QUESTION 9

WHO OR WHAT ARE THE MINERS?

There are nodes that, in addition to verifying network transactions and making sure that the Bitcoin rules are respected, have another feature: they work for the system and, specifically, they transcribe these transactions into the shared ledger called blockchain, making them irreversible.

But what do they do exactly?

We have said that Alice sends a transaction to Bob but that this, before reaching it, is "parked" in the temporary memory of the first available node.

These special nodes, called **miners**, draw transactions put into this temporary memory and transcribe them into a list called candidate block. Each miner creates his list of transactions and his candidate blocks.

Transcription is the simplest part of the miner's difficult job.

The miner, in fact, takes part in a competition with other miners: the aim of this competition is to find the solution to a cryptographic problem that is difficult to solve but easy to verify. Extremely simplifying the concept - I invite you to read Antonopoulos' Mastering Bitcoin for the details of the procedure - they look for a number, an extremely complex code to find, which is the solution to this problem.

They need very powerful and expensive machinery to find this number. They proceed by trial and error with a method called "brute force"; they calculate the first number, test it and if it doesn't go well they discard it, they calculate the second, test it and if it's not good they discard it, and so on. The difficulty in finding this single correct number is such that a miner can find it on average every 10 minutes!

Imagine having a mathematical problem in front of you: instead of solving it using standard formulas, you go ahead by trial and error, because there is no formula that can easily provide you with the solution.

It's like when our brain has to do with multiplication tables or powers: initially the difficulty is low to the point that we can proceed by automatisms and by memory, but when the numbers increase we end up proceeding by trial and error, adding or multiplying.

Once the correct solution has been found, the miner inserts it into the block under construction together with the transactions: the number is the proof that the miner actually participated in the tender and is called "**Proof of Work**". Afterwards, it sends this block, now closed, to the network, so that it is verified by the other nodes.

Imagine the miner's Proof of Work and the verification by nodes as a mathematical equation.

Let's see a very simple example based on a system of equations:

$$\begin{cases} y = 2x \\ 4x + y = 12 \end{cases}$$

It solves this way:

$$\begin{cases} 4x + 2x = 12 \text{ and then } 6x = 12 \\ x = 2, y = 4 \end{cases}$$

We spent some time solving this equation - very little, to be honest -, but we take less time to verify it.

It will be enough to replace the two unknown quantities x and y with the newly discovered numbers within the initial system.

So finding the proof of work is difficult, verifying it's easy.

In addition to the proof of work and the transactions of some users, the miner also enters another transaction, this time a bit special: it is set up to send a certain amount of bitcoins to the address of the same miner, as a reward for the work done.

Where do these bitcoins come from?

They are partly new and partly made up of commissions paid by those who send a transaction. We will see later on what this means: for now we just have to understand that the bitcoins, assigned by the winning miner to themselves, are called **reward** and this is composed of new bitcoins (**subsidy**) and commissions (**fees**).

They are in fact assigned by the winning miner to himself.

But how many are these new bitcoins?

If the choice were free, the miner would try to assign himself the highest possible number of bitcoins while respecting only the total limit of 21 million.

Fortunately, the Bitcoin rules are strict and the allocation of new bitcoins is predictable.

At the beginning of the Bitcoin history, the miner could assign 50 bitcoins for each block. The difficulty in calculating the Proof of Work was very low, like a simple equation.

Consequently a miner with good hardware could find many PoW in one day and 50 bitcoins were assigned about every 10 minutes.

At the time the single bitcoin had no economic value and those who mined technically did it at a loss, only to keep the system working, out of altruism or out of conviction that the value of Bitcoin, and consequently of their bitcoins, would be recognized tomorrow.

Four years after the network started, something changed.

The number of new bitcoins assigned by the miner to himself was reduced by half.

Was this a self-imposed punishment?

No. The system is designed like this.

Every four years, in fact, the number of new bitcoins that a miner can assign to himself is reduced by half: in 2012 it became 25.

This so-called **Halving** reduces bitcoin inflation and, as a side effect, it tends to increase the value of the single BTC, because the units become more scarce.

In 2016 the subsidy for miners went down to 12.5 per block, in 2020 it will be 6.25, in 2024 it will be 3,125, and so on.

What happens if the miner assigns more bitcoins than are foreseen by the system?

Very simple. The block would not be accepted; the nodes would consider it invalid because it did not respect the rules of the network.

You can't cheat.

What if the miner assigned himself less bitcoins than they owe?

It seems impossible, because the mining systems are automated, but this has already happened.

In 2011, a miner, known by the nickname of Midnightmagic, assigned to himself 49.99999999 bitcoins instead of 50 as a subsidy for a block he discovered.[19]

That unassigned satoshi is considered lost forever, because no one can assign more bitcoins than those established by the network rules. If Midnightmagic had assigned himself 50.00000001 bitcoins, he would have invalidated the block.

Paradoxically, if the miners began to assign themselves less bitcoins than they deserve, the BTCs in circulation would be reduced and the value per unit would increase.

In short, to Midnightmagic and to all those who make certain mistakes we say: *"Sorry for your loss, thank you for the deflation."*

What happens to the other miners who lose the race?

The miner who guesses the correct number, the solution to the cryptographic problem on which all the miners were working and competing, wins the chance to "close" the block, insert it in the blockchain with the benefits described above.

What do the other miners do?

The other miners are nodes too (or they rely on them), therefore they receive the block containing the solution and they verify it.

If the block is valid, they immediately stop working on the solution to the previous problem and start working on a new problem, contained within this same block.

The miner who guessed the answer to the previous riddle and proposed the new cryptographic problem does not know the solution and can therefore also participate in the new tender.

There is no possibility to cheat and insert in the block cryptographic problems of which the answer is already known!

Can miners work together to share profits?

Absolutely yes!

The mining difficulty is now very high. Miners need very powerful machines and in large numbers to be able to have some chance of finding the correct proof of work and getting the reward.

This necessity meant that Bitcoin mining became a real industry and large professional mining centers were created.

However, this does not mean that the non-professional user is cut off from the system.

For some years now, in fact, many amateur miners, in addition to investing a certain amount of money in the purchase of specialized mining machinery called ASICs, have decided to collaborate with each other, creating coordinated groups.

These groups are called Mining Pools: the node of the Pool receives, like all nodes, the block containing the cryptographic problem and its software divides the problem into many small packages that it sends to the various miners connected to it.

They process their part of the problem and send the results to the Pool. When a miner discovers the correct solution, the reward goes to whoever manages the Pool and this shares it among all the participants in a fair way, based on the power provided by each, in addition to keeping a part of the prize as a commission (fee).

Let's say I am a miner and participate in a Pool that has 100 participants and a 1% fee.

My hardware contributes 5% of the total power.
If I find the solution to the cryptographic problem I get 5% of the reward to which the owner of the Pool has taken 1% as his profit.
I prefer to mine along with others because I would never have discovered the solution by myself: I would have had to solve a problem that was too big and difficult, while cooperating with other miners I had to solve many smaller and simpler problems at a time.

QUESTION 10

HOW WILL THE MINERS SURVIVE WHEN ALL THE BITCOINS WILL BE MINED?

The reduction of the subsidy due to the miner decreases inexorably and will end.

It is not possible to proceed with infinite halving and the famous limit of 21 million bitcoins has been imposed as total supply.

It is estimated that after the 32nd halving the subsidy for miners will be 1 single satoshi per block, while there will no longer be any new satoshi from 2140.

Then what incentive will the miners have to continue to mine?

When a miner builds a block, he chooses transactions from various users and inserts them into his list (his **candidate block**).

However, these transactions contain another monetary incentive, called **mining fee**.

Each user can establish a commission in order to entice the miner to include his transaction in the first available block.

Let's imagine that Alice wants to send 1 bitcoin to Bob: to make sure the transaction reaches Bob as soon as possible she decides to include in the latter a commission of 10,000 satoshis. Alice will then send 1.0001 bitcoins to Bob, including 1 for Bob and 0.0001 for the miner.

It can be deduced that the miner will want to create blocks with transactions containing generous fees, leaving the lower commission transactions to the following blocks.

The total reward that will be up to the miner who wins the mining competition will therefore be X new bitcoins + Y bitcoins already in circulation, where Y is the sum of all the transaction fees inside the block under construction.

Let's take a practical example.

A miner, one day in 2019, creates a candidate block in which there are 500 transactions, with an average of 1,000 satoshis as a fee per transaction.

His reward will be 12.5 bitcoins (new, subsidy) + 500,000 satoshis already in circulation (fees), or 12.50500000 bitcoins.

If the single bitcoin is worth 10,000 USD, the reward for this block will be 125.050 USD.

With the reduction of the reward in new satoshis the role of the mining fees will be increasingly important.

For this reason it is assumed that miners will give an increasingly high priority to transactions containing a higher fee.

Apparently this could be bad, because it would force Alice to spend ever higher amounts to pay Bob. In fact, if you remember, we said that the main purpose behind the creation of Bitcoin was to have a decentralized monetary system whose transactions were irreversible.

The characteristic decentralization of the system and its security must be paid.

Does this mean that it is impossible to use Bitcoin to perform micro-transactions?

Let's say that, at the beginning, Bitcoin was a cheap monetary system, useful to reduce the costs deriving from the presence of a reliable third party in the classic digital monetary system. The reason is simple.

The price per single unit was negligible, even less than 1 USD, and the value of the single satoshi was not even calculable.

It could therefore be used in micro-transactions because, if the cost of 1 kg of bread was 3 bitcoins (or 3 USD), you could afford to spend 0.0001 bitcoins of commissions (in the example 0.0001 USD).

However, after a short period of time it was clear that a system, in order to be decentralized, safe and also cheap, must somehow scale.

If the single bitcoin is worth a lot, the fees also increase in value considering the same amount of satoshis spent. If then the miners' reward decreases, in addition to having the value of the fees on the rise, the satoshis necessary to speed up the transactions also increase.

It is therefore necessary for the system to scale up; that is to say that it adapts to the greater quantity of transactions and to the lesser quantity of new bitcoins for the miners, and that consequently allows to reduce the price per transaction rather than increase it over time.

The first solution, suggested by Nakamoto himself, was to increase the number of transactions that could be inserted into each block, by means of an increase in the size occupied by the block itself within the blockchain (block size).

In fact, Satoshi had inserted a limit to the block size (1 MB), to prevent the Bitcoin network from being filled with spam transactions at the beginning of its history, and consequently blocked, immediately losing its usefulness as an alternative payment system.

If this change had been made to the protocol and this limit had been removed or made variable, however, two serious problems could have occurred: the first, already mentioned, would have been the possibility of inserting spam transactions inside the blockchain, increasing the weight of the latter and slow down the network. But not only; miners would have been allowed to cheat.

A miner could in fact have generated false transactions for the sole purpose of quickly filling the block and arriving first at the Proof of Work, securing the prize.

The race to increasingly large blocks would have resulted in the creation of potential spam blocks as mentioned before, which would have been increasingly difficult to verify and would have required ever higher disk capacity to be stored.

As a hardware race took place by the miners to mine 1 MB blocks with increasingly high difficulty, so a specialization would also have occurred in the block verification.

Today anyone using low-performance hardware can verify transactions. In a reality where the blocks have no size limits, instead, only a few nodes would remain active.

Decentralization would become a utopia.

In short, even Satoshi is wrong.

But there is another method to increase the number of transactions while making them less expensive and maintaining decentralization of the system.

This method consists of using the Bitcoin network with its blockchain as a base layer to guarantee decentralization and irreversibility of transactions, and create layers above it in which to exchange value directly between peers, without resorting to a mining procedure.

The first and most famous Bitcoin second layer is called Lightning Network and we will explore it in the dedicated chapter.

This multi-level approach, which uses Bitcoin as a "static" network, whose modifications to the protocol are rare because the ultimate goal is to preserve decentralization, is the basis of the concept of LNP/BP, which we will clarify, also in this case, in a specific chapter.

Keep in mind, however, that claiming that most Bitcoin transactions have to move to a secondary layer in order to scale, does not mean that in the future the size of the blocks cannot or should not even be increased!

We should simply proceed with a cautious approach in order to preserve the decentralization level achieved by Bitcoin, aiming to saturate the basic network until there is actually a need for on-chain scaling solutions - never adjust what works - and above all develop fully second layers that can be used at full power maybe in ten or twenty years, but will be efficient, safe and available to billions of individuals and machines.

Giacomo Zucco's note: "Actually, the adoption of SegWit has led to what, to simplify, we could define an increase in the capacity of the blocks.
The block size is always around 1 MB, while the block weight, a new parameter introduced with the SegWit soft fork, can reach 4MB.
For more information, I invite you to read the *Understanding Segwit Block Size* article by Jimmy Song.[20]"

QUESTION 11

How do you make a transaction?

Bitcoins, intended as coins in the classic sense of the term, do not exist: when bitcoins are exchanged, a public register is actually updated which certifies the ownership (the blockchain), signing transactions with your private key, the only data actually in your possession. So, you don't move bitcoins but update their ownership.

To understand the operation of the model used by Bitcoin to send the "coins", I recommend reading Mastering Bitcoin by Andreas M. Antonopoulos, which explains precisely the concept of output and input of a transaction and how this is technically carried out in all its phases.

Here we will see instead how these transactions are carried out from the user's point of view, above all of the one who is a beginner or wants to immediately exchange money.

Transactions on blockchain

Blockchain transactions are currently considered to be classic transactions and constitute the vast majority of bitcoin movements within the system.

In the future these transactions will most likely be performed on special layers built on top of Bitcoins, called "transaction layers". In the chapters *What is Lightning Network?* and *Comparison between TCP/IP and LNP/BP* I explain better what is meant by this definition.

Let's see how these classic transactions are carried out.

For this example I will use the Edge wallet by Airbitz Inc. but the steps are almost the same for Bitcoin Core or for any other type of wallet you choose to use.

Let's say that Alice wants to send 1 bitcoin to Bob and intends to execute a transaction on blockchain.

Alice will open her BTC wallet in which she has funds and will click on Send.

Here she will have to enter Bob's public address and specify the amount to send to him.

If you remember, in the chapter *Who created Bitcoin?* we talked about public keys and private keys.

Bob's public address is an alphanumeric string derived from his public key: you can imagine the public address as an IBAN.

Example of public address 39EVqFcspspQRgNKPuugsbGrn5NN5QvUT9

When you make a wire transfer with your bank, you insert the name and surname (or company name) and the IBAN in the recipient field, to be sure that the funds actually go to the right recipient.

In Bitcoin it is as if we were using a disposable IBAN, which is a public address that we will change from time to time for security and privacy reasons.

Now Alice will see that, by setting 1 BTC as the amount to send, the application will calculate a mining fee that Alice will have to pay.

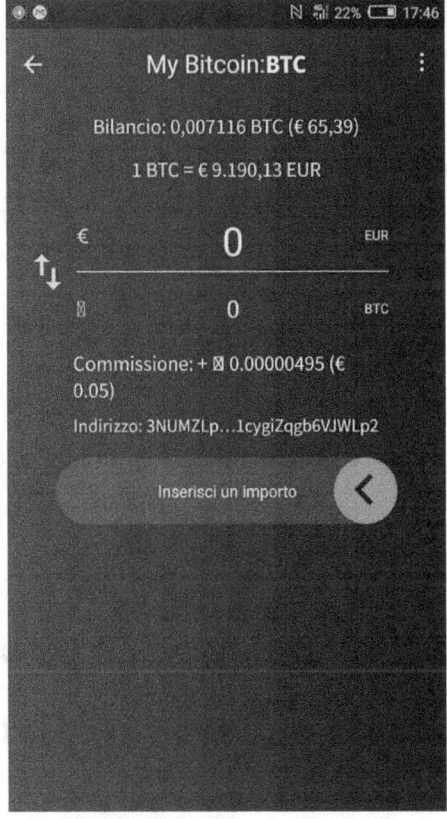

This sending commission is paid to the miners who will enter the transaction in the Bitcoin blockchain (see chapter *Who or what are the miners?*).

This fee is a value that the user can establish: the higher it is, the greater the chance that the transaction will be inserted in the first available block and that it will therefore be confirmed quickly.

Alice in this case uses a good wallet and therefore can choose for herself how much to pay to the miners. Since she is in no hurry and Bob can wait 1 day for confirmation of the transaction, Alice decides to pay a low commission.

Everything I describe now runs in the background without showing it to the user, so don't be afraid, the process is much simpler and faster.

> Let's assume that the 1 BTC transaction carried out by Alice to Bob will weigh 250 bytes on the Bitcoin blockchain and that Alice, by clicking on Low Commission, indirectly determines to spend 5 satoshis per byte. The application will calculate the commission that Alice will have to pay by simply multiplying 5 * 250 bytes.

When Alice moves to the send screen, she will see that, for a 1 BTC transaction, she will have to pay 1,250 satoshis, or 0.00001250 BTC. In total, therefore, he will pay 1.00001250 bitcoins, of which 1 to Bob and 0.00001250 to the miner who will insert the transaction in the blockchain.

Why do you have to pay a commission when you send money?

When you make a digital payment you are probably used to thinking that transactions do not involve service fees: actually, when you pay with your credit/debit card, these commissions are covered by the recipient of the payment, for example the shopkeeper from whom you buy shoes.

You should not think of transactions on Bitcoin as an alternative to those on Visa, Mastercard circuits etc.

I used the term IBAN when I talked about a public address and I did it with full knowledge of the facts.
Basic Bitcoin transactions (via blockchain) are much more similar to international transfers.

Indeed, if compared to transfers between countries that do not have consolidated commercial relationships or that are not in the same free trade area (eg. EU), Bitcoin transactions are much cheaper!

Alice now reviews the transaction and authorizes it if she thinks the commissions are acceptable. If a transaction of this type were made while I was writing, Alice would have the possibility of transferring an equivalent value of around 10,000 dollars by paying a commission of 12.5 cents. I would say more than cheap!

Then, if we consider that Bob could be in any part of the planet, even several hours away from Alice, and would probably receive this large amount of money in less than a day and in total autonomy, I would say that the advantages of Bitcoin compared to the classic digital systems are obvious.

Bob receives 1 bitcoin from Alice and can spend it because he can sign future transactions with the private key corresponding to the address that received the funds: he can prove that he is the owner of that address and he has the right to move the money.

From a user perspective, the process is much simpler. If Bob wants to spend that money, he can do it the same way as Alice.

His wallet will perform a procedure that will not be shown to Bob and which I will explain very briefly below.

Once these funds are received, the wallet will show them "on arrival" but not yet confirmed. After some time the transaction will be written in the blockchain and then the wallet will show them "confirmed".

Bob will be able to spend these funds even when they are in the "on arrival" state, but let's say he needs to spend them a few days after their confirmation.

Bob's wallet contains the private key corresponding to the public address he used with Alice: when Bob wants to spend his bitcoins, the wallet will sign the transaction with this private key, effectively authorizing payment, because it will show that he can move the funds. Only this private key can carry out transactions with the funds of that public address.

If you think about it, this is similar to what happens with the public key cryptographic system (RSA) for sending an encoded message on an unsafe channel. With the RSA system, Alice will be able to encrypt the message with Bob's public key and send it publicly. Bob will be the only one able to read the content of the message because this will be decodable only thanks to his private key, which he jealously guarded (see *Who created Bitcoin?*).

The blockchain transactions have a very high level of security regarding the irreversibility of the same, but they require some time to be confirmed by the network and above all, as we have seen, they involve fees which can be very high and which will still be more, if we look at the equivalent value in dollars, if the price of the single bitcoin should increase again.

Transactions via Lightning Network

Lightning Network is a payment protocol that represents a second layer above the basic Bitcoin layer.

We'll go into it in the dedicated chapter, but for the moment let's see it this way: Bitcoin is the basic layer, the one that guarantees the security of the system and the irreversibility of the transactions, Lightning is a network of payment channels that guarantees scalability (can be performed millions of transactions per second against about 7 Bitcoin transactions on blockchain), speed (network confirmations have not to be expected), privacy (payments are made directly between two users) and convenience (no commissions are paid to the miners, indeed they could be have completely free transactions).

To hazard a comparison, Bitcoin is to international wire transfers as Lightning Network is to Visa and Mastercard.

Lightning Network, due to the absence of the role of miners in transactions, is very useful for micropayments, ie most transactions that take place in everyday life.

Let's say that Alice has to pay Bob, her trusted baker, 100 satoshis for 1 kg of bread.

Alice will need to use a wallet compatible with Lightining Network.

In this example Alice uses BlueWallet, but consider that this is a semi-custodial wallet, so if you want to try some transactions on Lightning Network using this wallet, make sure you don't keep too many satoshis in it. Advanced user can also use BlueWallet in a non custodial way, linked to their personal full node.

Bob will show the bill to Alice and, with his Lightning Network compatible wallet, will generate an **invoice** from 100 satoshis.

Alice will open her wallet: she will now scan the QR Code from Bob's wallet and click Send.

55

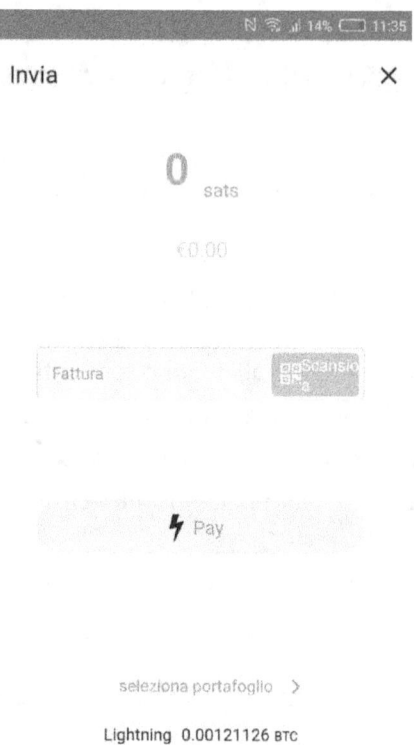

Done.

Bob will receive the funds in a few seconds and these will already be expendable in security, because they won't have to be transcribed on the Bitcoin blockchain.

You will have noticed that in this type of transaction it is not Alice who must directly establish how many satoshis to send and to which public address, but it is Bob who must create a unique invoice which, once paid, will no longer be reusable. The invoice will become unusable even if it is not paid after a few minutes from its creation.

Transactions on Lightning Network are currently still little practiced and the network is still under development; they have still a lower level of security than blockchain transactions in terms of their irreversibility, but they are faster, privacy-oriented and above all allow you to move even very small amounts of money without commissions or almost, which is not feasible with transactions on the base layer. They even allow you to make payments in sub-satoshi, effectively eliminating any future liquidity problems in the Bitcoin system (see chapter *The "danger" of deflation in Bitcoin*).

In the years to come, probably, much simpler wallets will be created that will automatically choose the type of transaction to be performed, with maximum savings in time and fees for the user.

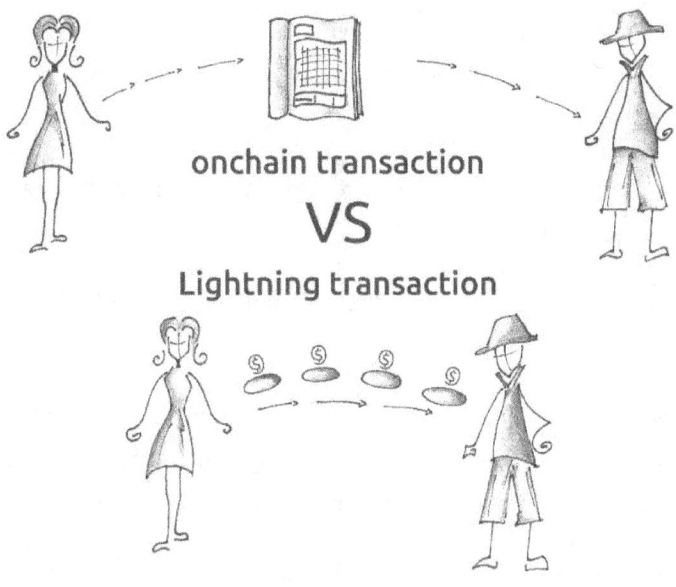

QUESTION 12

How do I store bitcoins?

Even if you don't really own files called bitcoins but rather a sort of "ownership certificate" that allows you to set these "digital coins" in motion, we can simplify by saying that bitcoins are stored in an electronic wallet. The wallet can be represented by an application on your smartphone or software on your computer. This application contains your public addresses, that are alphanumeric strings, through which you can "receive" bitcoins (analogous to the well-known banking IBAN), and private keys, to be kept hidden (similar to your bank credentials).

The private key certifies your property, so if you lose that you cannot recover your bitcoins.

Through the private key, your wallet can calculate the spendable budget and can have new transactions verified.

The vast majority of wallets do not show the user the private keys to prevent the latter from sharing them, but if they are non-custodial wallets they allow the owner to export them and save them elsewhere.

Some users prefer to keep their funds on wallets that do not allow this private key backup: these are called custodial wallets and are centralized systems, analogous to classic banks but often with a much less efficient security system than the latters.

QUESTION 13

WHAT IS A BITCOIN FORK?

In computer science, the term fork refers to the development of software based on the source code of a previous project.

In Bitcoin there are different types of forks: we consider **soft forks**, **Consensus hard forks** and **hard forks without Consensus**.

Soft forks are made to introduce a new functionality to the Bitcoin protocol while preserving the retro compatibility of the new version.

The most important soft fork of the last period concerns the introduction of SegWit (or Segregated Witness), whose main purpose was the resolution of the problem of malleability[21] of Bitcoin and that, as a secondary effect, "streamlined" the weight of transactions within the block.

There are no compatibility problems: non-SegWit wallets, whose addresses typically start with 1, can send bitcoins to SegWit addresses, recognizable because they start with number 3 or with bc1, and SegWit wallets can send BTC to non-SegWit addresses.

Consensus hard fork

Hard forks driven by the Consensus of the community are typically performed for the resolution of serious flaws in the code or for the introduction of a new feature not compatible with the previous code.

Let's assume that in the future will be necessary to increase the size of the Bitcoin blocks to increase the scalability on blockchain, ie the number of transactions for each individual block. Those who propose this change will seek to obtain the Consensus from the network nodes.

The change could initially be welcomed and the developers could write new versions of the software containing this increase in block size (eg a new version of Bitcoin Core).

Now the "vote" passes into the hands of those who maintain the nodes: if they accept the change, they will install the new version of the application, otherwise they will continue to use the current version, rejecting it.

When the nodes start installing the new software, the "right to vote" passes to the miners.

A date will be established in which the changes will become operative and the miners will have to choose which chain to mine: either the main one, without modification, or the new fork. The chain that will gain more computing power will be considered the main one.

If therefore the fork will have the support before the community of developers, then of the nodes and finally of the miners, then it will have gained the Consensus and called "main chain".

It goes without saying that if one of these "entitled to vote" were missing, the fork would fail.

Hard fork without Consensus

Technically speaking, a hard fork without Consensus does not exist and is simply defined as a failed fork.

In fact, only the bifurcations that took place successfully, and therefore in agreement with the Consensus, are defined by the developers as "Hard Fork".

Nodes have the highest level of importance in Bitcoin: if a hard fork is supported by the miners but rejected by the majority of nodes, it is highly probable that the bitcoin asset of the original chain would maintain a higher economic value than that of the initially longer and with more computing power secondary chain. The decrease in the new chain's bitcoin value would have repercussions on the miners, who would have less profit to continue to mine this blockchain and would therefore be forced, for economic interest, to shift their computing power over the previous one.

A recent example occurred with a Bitcoin Cash fork, also a Bitcoin fork that took place without Consensus. The new chain called BSV initially had more hashrate (computing power) than the old BCH (Bitcoin Cash) and its chain remained the longest for a few days. The majority of the Bitcoin Cash nodes however did not support the new fork and this led to a significant decrease in the price of the new BSV assets, with consequent huge economic losses on the part of the miners.

Now the Bitcoin Cash chain is again the longest, has more hashrate than that of BSV (more than double) and the asset has a market dominance of about 2% against 0.9% of BSV.

Clearly both these forks, having taken place without Consensus, do not represent the main Bitcoin chain, whose BTC asset has a market dominance of about 70%.

We said that Bitcoin is an open source project and that anyone can use the code for many different purposes.

We have also said that when the Consensus is not respected and the modifications to the protocol are carried out anyway, these, despite being rejected by the majority of Bitcoin nodes, create a fork to the code, called hard fork without Consensus.

What does this mean for us Bitcoin supporters (the main chain) and for our bitcoins?

Absolutely nothing.

The original chain is not affected by the changes and our bitcoins remain safe.

What happens is that the chain splits, a new chain is generated and this continues its path independently of Bitcoin.

It may happen that, if the modification project involves the creation of a new chain in competition with the previous one, a new asset is created: in the case of the non-Consensus fork of 2017, the bitcoin cash asset (BCH) was created.

Bitcoin holders suddenly found themselves in possession of two assets: bitcoin (BTC) and bitcoin cash (BCH). The first maintained its economic value, the second lost value compared to the first.

However, users had the opportunity to decide whether to keep both assets, sell one in favor of the other or simply ignore the second.

Personally I decided to support only the main chain and to respect the Consensus, so I sold my few BCH satoshis in favor of my precious good satoshis (BTC).

Giacomo Zucco's note: "The analogy with a vote, however suitable to provide an understandable image of the complex dynamics of Consensus to non-expert readers, is certainly simplistic and should not be taken too literally. The choices made in the software development phase do not take place through a "democratic" vote, but with a complex merit-based process similar

to those typically adopted by many open protocols (for example the Internet itself), based on concepts such as the "rough consensus" and described in part, for example, in the article by Jameson Lopp *Who Controls Bitcoin Core?*.[22] Even the so-called "vote" of the nodes should not be considered as such in the literal sense, for example due to the fact that the mere "number of nodes" does not represent a verifiable metric (the true metric, which can only be reconstructed ex-post and is not strictly quantifiable, concerns the economic weight of an institution that receives funds using a Bitcoin node for validation). Finally, even the so-called "vote" of the miners, as far as the relative hashrate represents, unlike the "number of nodes", an objective and measurable metric, does not represent at all a "democratic" decision process, but is instead properly intended as a "signaling of readiness" mechanism, with purely technical connotations, even if there have been attempts to portray it as a "political" vote."

QUESTION 14

HOW DO I RECOGNIZE THE FALSE BITCOINS BY THE TRUE ONES?

Those who want to follow a new chain will be able to do so, but if they try to send alternative bitcoins to the main chain these would not be recognized as valid.

In fact, this is a way to distinguish between "real" and "fake" bitcoins and is similar to what happens in centralized payment systems.

The USD chain can be split if a state adopts the dollar and then creates its own local currency.

The sharing of the name, even if the same "chain" is not initially shared, often happens in the monetary sphere: think of the Zimbabwe Dollar whose value is not even remotely comparable to the US Dollar, or, without going to the other side of the world, to the Canadian Dollar, which is worth about 0.76 USD.

Therefore it is easy to recognize different dollars, but it can be complicated to distinguish fake dollars even if they always seem USD:
with Bitcoin this cannot happen because any false bitcoins are simply not accepted by the network.

QUESTION 15

WHAT IS THE BLOCKCHAIN?

Technically speaking, **the blockchain is the ledger of validated blocks of the Bitcoin protocol.**

Now we need to go deeper, because it is a difficult concept to understand, since most of us are used to cash transactions in the real world and, when it comes to digital transactions, it is not clear how these happen.

Let's see together how digital transactions take place and how we arrived at the definition of blockchain mentioned above.

If you remember the example about the transaction between Alice and Bob, we said that in classic digital transactions there is a third party that authorizes the payment.

Well, what it does, in short, is nothing more than updating the internal register containing Alice's movements and sending the update request to Bob's bank, which will update the balance of the latter.

Therefore, there are no files (or tokens) transferred between one bank and another, much less cash transferred physically from one party to another by means of a delivery service.

These are pure and relatively simple numerical ledgers.

So, let's come to the blockchain, a register that do not need the reliable third party, and analyze it.

A very first definition of blockchain could be the following: a distributed and decentralized list of digital data inserted respecting a temporal order.

You will understand well that I have told you everything and nothing.

What data? A distributed list between whom? How decentralized? Which temporal order is and established by whom?

In short, such a definition raises more questions than answers.

A distributed ledger

The concept of distributed ledger (**DLT, Distributed Ledger Technology**) is very generic and refers to a technology that allows data to be stored in a distributed way, avoiding centralization on a single large server, which if attacked could lead to the fall of the entire system and the consequent loss of the data itself.

Distributed Ledger technology is decentralized in data management but does not necessarily imply decentralization of the organization that adopted or created it. Potentially, it can already be used by your bank.

The chain of blocks

The concept of "chain of blocks" (later become time chain, then block chain and finally blockchain), was introduced by Satoshi Nakamoto in 2008, in his document *"Bitcoin a peer-to-peer electronic cash system"* [1]: to ensure that a completely digital monetary system could exist that could not be attacked by third parties, such as hackers, governments and private institutions, it was necessary to find a way to decentralize network management and the issuance of monetary units. It was also necessary that the new system did not allow the user to spend the same money several times, just as it is not possible for the same person to pay twice with the same banknote.

But I am repeating myself because we have already seen, in the first chapters, what Bitcoin is and why it was created.

So here is the idea of using a "block" validation system.

We have already seen that the block is created by a miner and is, in essence, the set of some transactions made by the users, a transaction that pays the miner for the work done and the Proof of Work he discovered.

But the block has something more inside it:

- **a sort of index that links it to the previous block**
- **the problem that the miners will have to solve and that will be linked to the next block.**

We simplify by imagining the block as the page of a book that has thousands more pages.

If this has not a page number and is removed from the book along with others, it would be difficult if not impossible to put it back in its place, to understand the reading order.

The blockchain is just like a book and the blocks, temporally ordered, constitute its numbered pages.

Through this book we can monitor all the transactions made by the participants, make sure that no one cheats, for example spending twice the same money, and even go back to the very first transaction, contained within the first block, called Genesis Block, made by Satoshi Nakamoto.

Side note but of fundamental importance.

There is no blockchain without Bitcoin!

The blockchain is only a part of the Bitcoin Protocol, which is the set of all the protocols and different technologies.

The base layer Bitcoin Protocol does not work without blockchain as it does not work without digital signatures, cryptographic keys, Proof of Work, nodes, etc.

However, we can exchange bitcoins (the currency of the system) even without resorting to the blockchain, or better, using that only for a small part, thanks to the so-called transaction layers, such as Lightning Network.

The blockchain, in a sense, is inefficient by design.

Its purpose is not to allow fast and free transactions but to ensure their irreversibility (or the tendency to irreversibility) and provide a temporal order to the blocks that contain them.
Each block must be communicated and verified by all the nodes of the network, which complicates things with regards to scalability and speed of transactions.

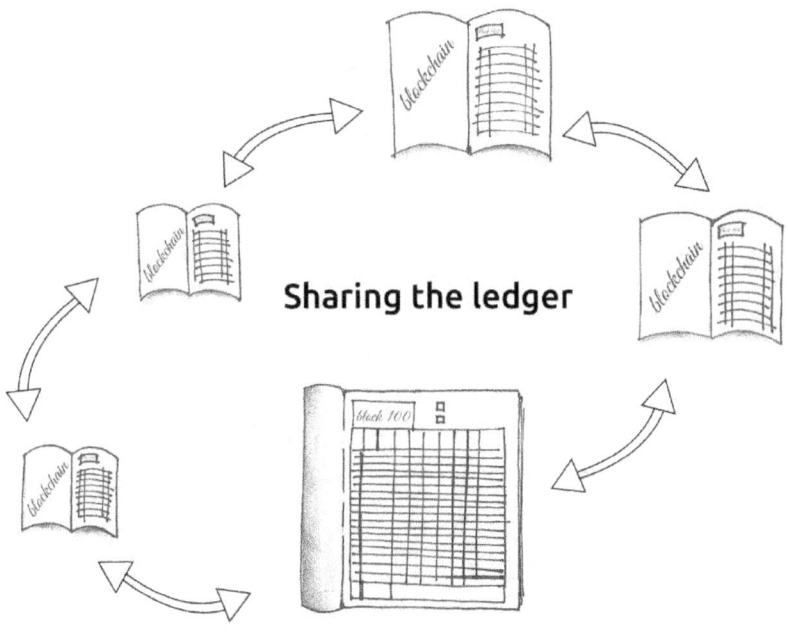
Sharing the ledger

Furthermore, this ledger, being public, does not lend itself to the anonymity of transactions, since these are clear and visible to all participants.

When someone tells you that Bitcoin is chosen as a payment system by criminals because of its anonymity, it actually says something that is not true.

Bitcoin is pseudo-anonymous: the blockchain keeps track of the Bitcoin transactions and addresses involved. They are, as mentioned, alphanumeric addresses and not names, so it is assumed that transactions take place anonymously for this reason. In reality, when a user makes his address public, he loses anonymity, unless he conceals his identity behind a nickname.

For example, if I need to receive a payment through the public address 39EVqFcspspQRgNKPuugsbGrn5NN5QvUT9 and I associate it with my name and surname, all transactions related to that address could be traced by anyone who wanted to carry out investigations.

QUESTION 16

WHAT ARE THE OTHER POSSIBLE USES OF THE BITCOIN BLOCKCHAIN?

The Bitcoin blockchain was created with the express purpose of establishing a transaction log, or rather a ledger of validated blocks containing transactions, which would allow all participants to keep track of their funds, avoid (or try to avoid) double spending of the latter and have an independent time reference.

To avoid double spending and to agree everyone on who has what.

Its function is therefore to certify that a certain transaction has taken place in a specific point in time and that it can be used only by those who own the private key relative to the public address to which the funds of that transaction are destined.

For this reason, one of the first names given to this block chain was time chain (or timechain).

Extremely, the blockchain is nothing but a register that changes over time and does not come back (or at least should not), not a revolutionary technology.
The revolution is in HOW this ledger is updated and by WHO.

Bitcoin, intended as a base layer and the set of protocols also containing the blockchain, in addition to all the other technological innovations that we have described above, is the real revolution.

Often those who use the term we are talking about do so out of context and therefore think that anything and every data can be put into a blockchain:

from personal information to products information, from the results of an election to the algorithms that make an AI, or a car, work.

Basically a blockchain is used to carry data regarding monetary transactions. It is precisely the monetary incentive to make the system work, and the highest possible incentive is represented by the bitcoins that circulate in it.

What incentive would you have to install on your PC a useful program to make a decentralized network work if not the monetary one? Certainly there are those who would be willing to maintain a decentralized network for academic or civil interest, assuming that there was a decentralized network for scientific research or electronic voting, but the number of participants (also called "nodes") would be clearly smaller than the ones in Bitcoin.

Having said that, which I repeat as a mantra to those who speak to me about "The Blockchain" and/or exalt it ignoring Bitcoin, let us now see what other possible uses this register could have.

Does the fact that the data is transaction information imply that it is not possible to use this register for anything else?

Absolutely not.

A transaction is made up of a series of information: in addition to the amount of bitcoins that are sent and those that are received as a change, assuming that it is a basic transaction from one address to another such as that seen previously between Alice and Bob, there is another parameter called OP_RETURN: within this parameter we can insert information (limited).

Why should we need to insert non-monetary data on a decentralized system like Bitcoin?

In short, for safety reasons: security of conservation, non-tampering and non-censorship.

It's not to get that data to its recipient as soon as possible, since the block containing the transaction, which in turn contains this additional information, must be processed by all nodes on the network.

Secondly, to avoid building a new blockchain for each new use case, given that there would probably be servers deployed in the hands of a few actors (permissioned) or an effectively decentralized (permissionless) network but not as safe as Bitcoin's.

If you remember we said that, to ensure the highest level of decentralization, it is necessary among other things that the registry is as light as possible: it follows that the data that we could insert in the Bitcoin blockchain will be relatively few compared to those that other distributed ledgers may contain, but will make them poorly decentralized.

So **the choice is between safety and performance**, intended as speed and storage capacity.

When my niece was born I inserted the message "*date XXXXXX, 22.00, Arianna was born!*" in the Bitcoin blockchain, in order to have a memory of that day in the future. Several blocks have passed since then, so I can say with relative confidence that this message will remain forever in the shared ledger.

I used the Bitcoin network to transmit a data not related to a monetary transaction.

The fact of having entered this message in the blockchain, however, does not mean that it corresponds to the truth!

I could have written a different date than the birth date, a different name or other conflicting or non-relevant information.

This message constitutes useful and real information for me, and is therefore a totally subjective certification.

When we write in the Bitcoin blockchain data other than monetary transactions, we simply go to insert a record and protect it from changes over time caused by external agents (a central body, an attacker, etc.). **We certify the data, but this does not mean that the information entered corresponds to reality.**

We therefore understand that the blockchain, even if it is useful to protect the digital data from future tampering, does not guarantee its truthfulness and therefore does not lend itself well, for example, to the control of a supply chain.

Do we want to insert the serial number of a car on a blockchain?

Let's do it, but remember that there will always be someone in charge of writing that data and therefore it will be able to tamper with the reality: in short, the sedan car drawn on the blockchain, could prove to be a beetle after the delivery.

This is because it is not an object of the material world but a digital counterpart to be transmitted on the distributed ledger. Someone will have to create this digital object, right?

Is the blockchain used for non-monetary purposes useless?
No.
There is also the possibility of creating objective certifications if the "timechain" property is used to fix a data over time for something that actually requires a so-called timestamp; in short, if it is used as a timestamp register.

In this case the certification is not provided by the entered data (subjective parameter) but by the time it was entered in the blockchain (objective parameter).

A practical example

Soundreef is an independent copyright manager (Independent Management Entity according to EU Directive 2014/26/EU) recognized by the United Kingdom Intellectual Property Office[23], in competition with SIAE (Italian Society of Authors and Publishers) that in Italy, until recently, had a monopoly in the management and collection of copyright.

Well, from November 2018 Soundreef uses the Bitcoin blockchain to certify the authorship of the songs composed by its artists.

Soundreef authors can use proprietary software to obtain a digital ownership certificate: this is associated with a unique **hash** that is inserted into a Bitcoin transaction, thus ending up in its blockchain.

If someone were to plagiarize, the original author could prove ownership of the song simply by retrieving the certificate that was temporally marked.

Let's take a specific example.

I am an author and I have the file (the digital certificate) of my work dated November 1st, 2019 and the associated hash inserted in the blockchain the same date. If someone registered a plagiarism, this will be given later to my digital certificate/hash couple on blockchain, therefore, in the legal venue, it will be easy to prove the violation of my intellectual property.

The same thing can happen in the case of registration of patents, and in all those areas in which to count is the first to register the idea; where therefore a "recorder" or "time marker" is needed.

It is not necessary to use a proprietary software, as in the example of Soundreef, but it is enough to create a digital document in whose metadata the creation date is present, generate a unique hash corresponding to that document and write this hash in the OP_RETURN of a Bitcoin transaction. It goes without saying that it is necessary to keep the original file and the corresponding hash. Without one of them we could not claim our property on the document, or rather, have it created and certified at a specific point in time.

To date, the only function of the blockchain other than monetary transactions is the temporal marking of a digital data, or temporal certification (timestamp).

Any other use is at least not appropriate, if not even fraudulent.

The famous "supply chain tracking" falls into these inappropriate uses and lends itself well to fraud.

The example of the apple

We have a NON-unique material object, an apple, which is "digitized" by a worker.

An Italian farmer sells its apples grown in compliance with the EU regulations to a large international distributor.

The distributor has business with many farmers and manages sales to shopping centers around Europe and North Africa. The products come from many different areas, some from the EU, others extra EU.

The distributor however uses "the Blockchain"!

The procedure is relatively simple: some workers collect the apples from the producers and apply a label, on which there is a QR code, on the cassettes. Other employees create digital objects containing information about the apples: date of harvest, origin, type of apples, etc. The QR code links these apples to the digital objects created by the workers and these are "inserted" into a blockchain (the marketing sector would say "within the Blockchain").

If in the meantime the employer has replaced the boxes of apples produced in Italy with fruits produced in Morocco, removing the stamp from the Italian boxes and applying it on the Moroccan ones, it does not matter: when we will present ourselves in front of the fruit counter of our trusted supermarket and with the smartphone we will scan the QR code, we will be happy, because we will know that our apple is the one produced and harvested in Italy.

Shout out to the supply chain tracking through the blockchain!

I would like to point out that I have nothing against Moroccan apples, which could be even better than Italian ones. They are simply not the same thing and in the illustrated example a food fraud is carried out.

Why did I specify "NOT unique object" at the beginning of the example?

Because in fact this is the only case in which the "transformation" of a material object into a digital object and consequent tracking through a blockchain, could work.

If it were possible to describe in detail the physical-chemical characteristics of a single object to the point of realizing a digital counterpart of it, then we could be sure that the object in front of us is actually the example traced using (also) a blockchain. However, this is a fantasy, as the "description" of the single object is susceptible to human error.

Let's take a painting by Leonardo: we can describe the features that make it unique with very high precision. We can take this data, associate a hash with it and put this into the Bitcoin blockchain.

However, if our analysis turns out to be fallacious and a fake appears that corresponds to the characteristics expressed by our analysis, the digital alter ego would represent the wrong painting and the tracking would go to hell.

In short, as long as we remain in the digital realm and use the Bitcoin blockchain as a time marker (for example the ownership certificates associated with a hash) then we make an alternative but useful use of it, if instead we move to the real world, we can do nothing but "track" a digital object while the real one could be counterfeited or not be original, in case of unique objects.

Bitcoin's detractors tend to consider the inherent limitations of its blockchain and its poor predisposition to alternative uses such as proof that Bitcoin represents a bad monetary system.

With gold you can do so many things, with Bitcoin you can't!

The fact is that Bitcoin was created with the express purpose of establishing an alternative monetary system. It has precise features and functions.

If over time we will find alternative functionalities to the simple exchange of value among peers without a reliable third party, it is not known and is not even important right now.

Gold does not owe its value to the alternative uses that can be made of it, but to its scarcity which makes it a good Store of Value; it has been a precious metal for centuries, even before discovering its electrical conductivity and opening the field to its many uses in the technical/scientific field.

Some populations of South America, before the arrival of the European conquerors, possessed large gold reserves. Gold was mainly used as an ornamental material because it was malleable, resistant to corrosion and above all ... brilliant.

He had no monetary value among these populations, simply because it was not a scarce commodity. Pre-Columbian societies gave gold only a symbolic power mostly associated with the divinities of the Sun and, unlike Europeans, did not conceive it as a medium of exchange.

It is therefore clear that the value given to a good is completely subjective and extremely correlated to its scarcity.

If gold were not a scarce asset, its secondary uses would remain and perhaps increase in number, but its usefulness as a Store of Value and monetary medium of exchange would be lost.

Fortunately Bitcoin was designed to remain scarce and have the characteristics of a digital monetary medium.

Giacomo Zucco's note: "To date it is actually possible to obtain a "certain date" certification ("timestamping") even without writing ANY additional data on the Bitcoin time-chain, but by manipulating the data already entered

for a normal transaction. For example this is possible with the technique called "pay-to-contract" (in which a public key is manipulated to insert a commitment to a message), or with the one called "sign-to-contract" (in which one manipulates a signature). The first technique is the heart of all future Taproot-related innovation, as well as being the one we use for the RGB protocol. Both can be used as a "zero blockchain-footprint" alternative to the more traditional OP_RETURN, even in the context of the OpenTimeStamps library."

QUESTION 17

What is a Bitcoin node?

In IT, "node" indicates any hardware capable of communicating with other devices connected to the network.

In Bitcoin, things get a little more complicated.

Users can in fact interact with the Bitcoin network and each constitute a node by transmitting information relating to the transactions, even if in different ways.

There are different types of nodes, specifically: **full node, miner node** and **SPV client** (although some, including myself, struggle to consider these nodes).

Originally full node and miner node coincided. The miner needed to keep a copy of the entire Bitcoin blockchain in order to do his job and who, instead, just wanted to verify the transactions, could act on his node and disable the mining feature.

To coincide were not only full node and miner node but also the concept of node and wallet.

If at this point in the book you have clear how to store and send bitcoins, you will know that to execute transactions we need an electronic wallet.

The first ever wallet, which still runs on most Bitcoin online full nodes is the Bitcoin Core wallet, also called Satoshi Wallet, because it was developed directly by Satoshi Nakamoto. You can download it from the bitcoin.org website or from the GitHub repository.

Bitcoin Core is a full node software: to fully utilize it, you need to download the entire Bitcoin blockchain, which currently weighs about 250 GB. The blockchain can be downloaded in different ways: with the txindex disabled or enabled (txindex = 1), in Pruned mode or with this mode disabled.

What does it mean?

In Pruned mode, the user maintains a smaller version of the Bitcoin blockchain. The oldest data is deleted (eg old transactions not directly linked to your addresses). This means that you can save a lot of disk space: for example, we can decide to keep only 500 MB of data instead of the over 250 GB required by the entire blockchain.

If we download Bitcoin Core, we do not activate the Pruned mode and in the configuration file we insert the parameter txindex = 1, instead, we will download the entire Bitcoin blockchain plus the complete transaction index, that is the whole history of the transactions performed by the members of the network.

All of them!

Downloading the entire Bitcoin blockchain gives us a complete user experience that is perfectly in line with the philosophy behind the protocol: the possibility to completely and independently verify all transactions, without having to trust another node or other verification system, including the ability to influence the Consensus, because we could reject any changes to the Bitcoin rules by simply refusing to update the software to a version that contains them.

The verification is useful, among other things, to avoid accepting "double spending" transactions if the system has undergone a double spending attack or a hidden fork.

For the average user this can be an excessive precaution, but it allows you to actively influence the choices of the network.

Furthermore, for a company operating in the sector or for those who want to activate a Lightning network node, it is essential to have Bitcoin nodes that are always updated and contain the complete history of the network.

There are also other full node implementations, such as Bitcoin Knots, Libbitcoin or bitcoinj, just as there are different software for managing another decentralized network, used to share files rather than a transaction ledger: the BitTorrent network.

To guarantee decentralization of the system and its security, we should continue to maintain and develop different full node software.

As we have seen, a full node can weigh up to several GB, so it was necessary to develop solutions that would allow even those with limited resources, such as low memory capacity on the PC or poor Internet connection, or to anyone wishing to use mobile devices, to be able to manage Bitcoin transactions independently and without private keys "custody" by third parties.

For this purpose the SPV (Simplified Payment Verification) wallets, also called lightweight clients or light wallets, were developed.

QUESTION 18

WHAT IS A LIGHT WALLET?

Unlike a full node which, as mentioned, downloads all the blockchain or at least all the transactions of our addresses and keeps them in memory, an SPV client only downloads the headers of the blocks, not the part of data that concerns transactions.

I will briefly illustrate the structure of the block here, inviting anyone interested to learn more, to read Antonopoulos' Mastering Bitcoin.

If you find the text too complicated you can safely skip it and come back later, when you feel ready.

A block is divided into four major sections: **Block Size, Block Header, Transaction Counter** and **Transactions.**

For the moment it is enough to know that the "weight" of the block on the blockchain is mainly due to the transactions and, to a much lesser extent, to the Block Header. Transaction Counter and Block Size together occupy 5 to 15 bytes, a negligible amount.

Considering that on average in a block there are about 1500 transactions[24] whose weight is about 500 bytes each, while the block header takes up about 80 bytes, we deduce that, avoiding downloading transactions, you have a savings of considerable space, less than about 1000 times!

When needed, the SPV client verifies the transactions by relying on full nodes. We have said that the saving in terms of space is considerable, but this lower consumption of resources also involves a problem: the SPV wallet must indeed "trust" an external node, hoping that the node is updated and that it respects the rules shared by the network.
The SPV wallet cannot independently check all transactions and therefore

cannot verify that a Btcoin transaction has not been performed twice from the same address.

I know I'm frightening you a bit, but it is necessary to understand that, when moving large funds, it would be better to do it through your own full node, while for small figures, you can tolerate the risk and rely on a light wallet.

For this reason, the most common type of wallet today is precisely the SPV, also due to the increasing use of smartphones to manage daily Bitcoin transactions.

There are many SPV wallets, more or less complete, in a number decidedly greater than those full node.

I will list some but this list is incomplete and does not consider hardware wallets.

Desktop Wallet

- **Electrum:** the best known SPV desktop client. Recently a malware version of Electrum has prompted users to display their private keys, so download the wallet always from reliable sources (the Electrum website) and beware of imitations.

- **Wasabi:** a client developed in order to substantially increase transaction privacy and therefore bitcoin fungibility. Wasabi wallet uses a technique called CoinJoin, which combines many transactions from different addresses into one big transaction, and this makes it extremely difficult to link senders to recipients.

Mobile Wallet

- **Edge Wallet**: open source multicurrency wallet produced by Airbitz Inc. I actively collaborate with this company, therefore, in full conflict of interests, I highly recommend it.
Seriously, it's also a non-custodial wallet, so it allows you to export but also import private keys, and these are not managed or even seen by Edge creators (zero knowledge system). With Edge it is also possible to set customized Bitcoin nodes, which will be used by the app in order to download the Header. You can also use the full node you have on your PC.

- **Samurai Wallet**: a privacy-oriented mobile wallet for Bitcoin, with a very interesting function: the ability to send bitcoins offline, using an open source system for encapsulating transactions within text messages and messages sent on the txTenna mesh network. Samurai also has its own transaction mixing system, in order to increase user's privacy.

QUESTION 19

What is a hardware wallet? And a paper wallet?

Let's start with the **paper wallet.**

We said that a Bitcoin wallet is composed of two series of numbers: a public address and a private key, with which transactions are signed and funds are set in motion.

The bitcoins you receive do not physically reside in your wallet (your app on your phone or your desktop software), or anywhere else.

It simply keeps track of the various owners, ie the public addresses to which the bitcoins that run in the system have been sent, on the blockchain.

It can therefore be deduced that, as long as we have the private key associated with an address on which we received bitcoins, we could use them wherever we are and with any application that allows us to import the keys.

If the app we use allows us to export private keys, we can make a backup of them simply by writing them on a sheet of paper.

If instead the application does not allow us to export them, well, we change app.

A paper wallet is simply this: a sheet of paper or other medium on which we have written our private keys.
We will have to guard it carefully, away from prying eyes, because that sheet contains our wealth.

Hardware wallet

A hardware wallet is, as the name implies, a device that we can use in tandem with compatible software to confirm our transactions.

The device contains the private keys of our Bitcoin wallets: when we have to execute a transaction this is signed through our hardware wallet and the private key is never exposed.

If we use a hardware wallet, however, we must be aware that this tool is only an additional protection to our paper wallet.

In fact, during the configuration of the device, we will have to memorize on a sheet a series of words called **seeds**. These seeds make up our Master Private Key, so if we lose them we will no longer have access to our bitcoins in the event of a hardware wallet failure. As with the paper wallet, keep this sheet safe!

The most popular hardware wallets on the market are currently produced by Trezor and Ledger. Between the two companies I would recommend the devices produced by Trezor, because they have an entirely open source software; this gives the possibility to check that there are no backdoors in the private keys management system.

Ledger uses bank-level security systems, which effectively neutralizes some physical attacks against which Trezor cannot effectively defend itself, but at the cost of having an important part of closed code, that is not verifiable by independent developers and therefore potentially exposed to backdoors.

In addition to the two hardware wallets mentioned, Coldcard should also be considered, a very interesting hardware proposal that integrates a dedicated chip for storing the private key and provides the user with a "duress PIN code", ie a security code useful in case of physical attacks: if typed, the wallet will not give access to the user's funds, but to another wallet, on which the owner could have uploaded only a few satoshis. The attacker would therefore not have access to the main wallet.

Another interesting feature of Coldcard is the so-called "Brick Me" PIN, which instead, used in extreme cases, destroys the private key and makes the wallet completely useless.

QUESTION 20

WHO SETS THE VALUE OF 1 BITCOIN?

The value of the single bitcoin is established, as for the classic market, by buyers and sellers: it can therefore be said that **the value is given by the encounter between demand and supply.** No state or bank can establish or guarantee its value.

Think of auctions: millions of them are played every day in the world.

The most disparate categories of objects can be sold in these auctions, but they are typically scarce goods.

Well, how do you establish the price of one of these objects?

It can be estimated and provided with auction bases, but the true value will be established by offers made by the public.

For the bitcoin asset, things work in a similar way.

The places appointed to carry out these auctions are typically online exchanges but they can also be physical spaces where sellers and buyers meet. Those who sell bitcoins typically offer a price trying to achieve the highest possible profit, or sell at a price higher than that paid at the time of purchase, while buyer proposes an offer trying to get the most advantageous price.

When demand and supply meet, the instant bitcoin price is born.

There are places where these instant prices are collected and the average bitcoin price is obtained. The best known is *CoinMarketCap*, a site that collects the price of bitcoin and many other cryptocurrencies, but also marketcaps, daily volumes, circulating supply and other useful information.

Remember that, as a general rule, if the volumes are reduced, as well as the places assigned to the exchange, the price changes will be greater.

Volatility tends to decrease when volumes increase.

For this reason the value of the single bitcoin can undergo very important variations and for the moment the asset is considered high risk.

To better understand the concept of volatility and how it can be used to our advantage, I invite you to read the chapter *Why should I convert my savings into something so volatile?*

QUESTION 21

Can we change the Bitcoin's economic policy?

In the chapter in wich we analyzed the critical points of the current monetary system we have mentioned the economic policy behind Bitcoin, completely different from that of the current system, called fiat system (see glossary), and similar to that of the Gold Standard because it is also based on scarcity, even if digital.

In the following table we can observe the main differences between the current system (fiat) and Bitcoin.

Main features	FIAT SYSTEM	BITCOIN SYSTEM
MONEY TYPE	From 10 to 20% in paper cash. Majority digital	100% digital cash. No fractional reserve
SCARCITY	Unlimited supply. Subject to quantitative easing	Limited (capped) supply to $2{,}1 \times 10^{15}$ base units
INFLATION	Theoretically infinite. 2% as ideal annual target	Predictable, finite. 3.73% today (2019), 1.88% from 2020. Halved every four years
DURABILITY	Paper cash can be lost, destroyed, stolen. Digital money subject to hacking and seizure	Private key can be lost. Digital cash is unseizable, unhackable, undestroyable
ISSUE	Issued by the government and central bank system	Issued by the software according to the fixed rules of the network
CONTROL TYPE	Centralized. Controlled by political authorities	Decentralized. Controlled by no one. Verified by the nodes
ADOPTION	Imposed by force, by law and/or military power	Adoption on a voluntary basis
COUNTERFEIT	Cash subject to counterfeit, digital money difficult to counterfeit but subject to attacks	Impossible to counterfeit a private key
FUNGIBILITY	High fungibility with cash. Low fungibility with digital money, subject to seizure	Medium fungibility on blockchain. High fungibility with satoshi on second layers
DIVISIBILITY	Low, usually two decimal places	High, eight decimal places on the blockchain, even higher on second layers

MONEY TYPE: it indicates the form in which the money is presented. In the fiat system, 10 to 20% of the money is in the form of notes or metal coins, the rest is digital.

Central banks can make fractional reserves. If this reserve is limited to 10%, it means that out of 1,000 USD deposited, only 100 will be available in the form of banknotes for possible withdrawals. If we take the example of capital control in Greece in 2015, we see how this fractional reserve has manifested itself in moments of lack of liquidity in the banking system: tourists were warned in advance to bring enough cash to avoid being left without money. Bitcoin is 100% digital and no more money can be created than the software put into circulation.

SCARCITY: the issuance of currency is unlimited for the fiat system (subject to quantitative easing), while it is limited to 2.1×10^{15} basic units for Bitcoin, further divisible downwards.

INFLATION: inflation in the fiat system is theoretically infinite but as an ideal reference it has an annual 2%. Bitcoin inflation is predictable and limited. From 3.73% today (2019), it will drop to 1.88% starting from 2020. Inflation halves every four years and will become deflation from 2140.

DURABILITY: the durability of banknotes is limited: they can be lost, destroyed or stolen. The digital money of the fiat system is subject to hacking and seizure. In the Bitcoin system private keys can be lost, not coins. The system was created in order to be non-censurable, non-sequestrable, non-destructible.

ISSUE: fiat money is put into circulation by governments and central banks. Bitcoins are released by the software according to the rules of the network.

CONTROL TYPE: in the fiat system, control over money is centralized and political in nature, in Bitcoin it is decentralized and no one has direct control over the entry or transactions. Transaction blocks are verified by system nodes.

ADOPTION: in the fiat system the adoption is imposed by force through the law and/or military power. In Bitcoin the adoption is on a voluntary basis; no one can force you to accept bitcoins and nobody can stop you.

COUNTERFEIT: cash is subject to counterfeiting, digital fiat money is difficult to forge but is subject to third-party attacks. In Bitcoin it is practically impossible to discover a private key through third-party attacks and bitcoins cannot be counterfeited.

FUNGIBILITY: the fungibility of cash is high (except for "marked" banknotes), but is very bad in the fiat cashless system. In Bitcoin the fungibility is good on blockchain, excellent on second layer.

DIVISIBILITY: the divisibility in the fiat system is low, typically limited to two decimal places. In Bitcoin it is high, equal to eight decimal places. On second layer it is possible to use smaller digits than satoshi.

Bitcoin's economic policy has been well defined in the construction phase of the system. The fact of having set up the network in this way, even before starting with its Genesis Block, makes this economic policy its foundation. It should not be changed, otherwise the entire building will fall.

So the Bitcoin economic rules cannot be changed?

The only part of the apparently non-modifiable code is precisely that relating to Bitcoin's economic policy. When I explain Bitcoin in my country, I ask audience to imagine the Bitcoin Protocol as the Italian Constitution. The first part of our Costitution, Fundamental Rights, is not technically modifiable unless a civil war is made.
In Bitcoin, "civil war" means hard fork, an IT term that indicates the bifurcation of open source code by one or more developers that makes the new version not compatible with the previous one (see *What is a fork?*).

So, taking up the question, no, the economic rules of Bitcoin can be modified, but only by reaching Consensus (Consensus hard fork) or by performing a hard fork without the Consensus but with the consequent creation of another chain with other rules and coins.

Risky forecast?
This fork will fail.

Why?
If I told you that tomorrow you can have a monetary system with more bitcoins than you can have now but that the value of the single bitcoin will drop dramatically, would you support the change to economic policy?
I don't, because I don't want my purchasing power to diminish over time.
My node will provide support for the only chain whose economic policy has not changed.

Let me clarify this point with an example.

Let's pretend for a moment that I have 0.1 BTC, or 10 million satoshi - which is impossible, because all my satoshis have been lost in a boat accident - and that there is a limit of 21 million bitcoins as a total supply.
A modification to the Bitcoin protocol is proposed which aims to raise the limit to 21 billion.
My 0.1 bitcoins will remain the same but now they would be put into circulation 1000 times more bitcoins than before. My purchasing power would inexorably go down over time.
And if these 21 billion bitcoins were "coined" in the same timeframe as the current protocol, that is to say adding 3 zeros also in the amount of bitcoins released to the miners and ending in 2140, my purchasing power would be practically wiped out overnight.

My node would oppose this proposal.

How to?
Simple!
Avoiding to install the new software that contains the new emission rules and the new total supply.

FOCUS 1

The Spectre of Inequality in Bitcoin

Some economists complain about the possibility that a monetary system with a fixed quantity of units of value (fixed supply) is dangerous because the individual would tend to save, and this would increase his purchasing power over time. The system would therefore facilitate a certain inequality because those who "entered first" had the opportunity to do so by paying a lower price and have been able to save over a longer period of time, compared to those who entered later.

On the contrary, a monetary policy based on the issue of units of value over an unlimited time would reduce the tendency to save, because the individual units tend to lose value over time as well as the purchasing power of those who hold them believing to save. The reduction in savings, combined with the change in money supply (monetary inflation), which according to some economist changes only as a function of changes in production and population, would lead to a more equitable system.

The concept is interesting and deserves to be investigated.

With some clarifications though.

First of all, the Bitcoin issue is limited (capped), not simply fixed.
These two terms might seem synonymous but they aren't: the concept of fixed supply suggests that the units are limited but also not divisible and that they are all already in circulation.
We have seen that instead the emission occurs in a constant way over time but halves every four years (see halving).
We will see in the following chapter that, even on the fractionability of bitcoin, things are not like this: we can have as many units as we want by

simply splitting BTC, without varying the total amount of bitcoins in circulation (**capped supply**).

Furthermore, if we consider the current monetary system, we see that the creation of unlimited money allows those close to the issuing entities, for lobbying or similar political purposes, to benefit unfairly - yes, here unequally.
This inequality is also fueled by loans to businesses and, indirectly, to citizens, issued by banks.[25]

According to the economist prof. Richard A. Werner:

"Bank credit creation does not channel existing money to new uses. It newly creates money that did not exist beforehand and channels it to some use.... What makes this 'creative accounting' possible is the other function of banks as the settlement system of all non-cash transactions in the economy. ... Since banks work as the accountants of record – while the rest of the economy assumes they are honest accountants – it is possible for the banks to increase the money in the accounts of some of us (those who receive a loan), by simply altering the figures. Nobody else will notice, because agents cannot distinguish between money that had actually been saved and deposited and money that has been created 'out of nothing' by the bank"

It is also interesting to read the final closure of the paper *How do banks create money, and why can other firms not do the same? An explanation for the coexistence of lending and deposit-taking* by prof. Werner:

*"In this paper it was found that banks combine what are effectively very different operations, namely deposit-taking and granting of loans under one roof, because in this way they can invent new money in the form of fictitious 'customer deposits' when purporting to engage in the act of 'lending'.
It was found that the defining characteristic of banks is that they are exempt from the Client Money Rules[26], which prevent other firms from creating money in the same way. It was found that, in practise, only banks can issue money in this way. (...)"*

Another point to consider is that those who firmly support the fact that a capped supply involves inequality, often fall into a "logical trap" or false syllogism.

Let's go back to the hypothesis expressed at the beginning and expand it:
"I enter the system first, I spend less to buy the units of value, so I can buy more and I have more time to save.
It follows that those who come later will be able to purchase less units because they will spend more and I will therefore be able to lord and dictate the line of the economic system thanks to my "unjust" and amazing purchasing power."

In short, a feudal situation would arise.

The reasoning would seem logical but is fallacious on several points.

First of all it would presuppose a closed system, in which resources are well-stored and conserved and there is a coordination between the great "capitalists" able to control the purchasing power of individuals.
As if to say: *"we have a lot of money; let us agree so that the price of our precious good continues to increase artificially and new individuals are attracted to the system. But these will have to settle for the crumbs! "*.

In reality, the monetary system is open and subject to a free market.

Of course there are rich actors (**whales**) able to influence the market trend (the price), but not to coordinate a global control system worthy of the most grim conspiracy theory. It is easier for this to happen in the current fiat system, where the power to issue new currencies is in the hands of a few central banks and where the creation of money and direct control over large capitals coincide.

Fortunately, in Bitcoin those **who possess large amounts of assets cannot technically influence monetary policy because they would also be forced to control the majority of the nodes of the system.**

Secondly, it would presuppose that most of those who first entered the system already knew that the price of the single bitcoin would reach today's levels and that therefore they had spent nothing to be able to guarantee a huge purchasing power in the future. In short, all of them should be "**Hodlers**", regular savers.

Greg Schoen
@GregSchoen

I wish I had kept my 1,700 BTC @ $0.06 instead of selling them at $0.30, now that they're $8.00! #bitcoin

Traduci il Tweet
12:57 AM · 17 mag 2011 · Twitter Web Client

But we know that, in a free market, individuals buy and sell trying to make the highest profit. Many have immediately used Bitcoin as a monetary system for the purchase of goods; bitcoin was cheap, it had fast and practically free transactions. How many have bought or even mined so many bitcoins in the early days and now remain with few BTCs in their wallets?

In 2010, a year after the Bitcoin network started, the single bitcoin struggled to find a monetary value.

It was extremely difficult to find someone willing to sell a good or a service and to have in exchange those that at the time seemed only Monopoly money that anyone could produce with a simple personal computer.

On May 18, 2010, on the BitcoinTalk forum[27], a user called laszlo (Laszlo Hanyecz) sent a curious request to the community:

"I'll pay 10,000 bitcoins for a couple of pizzas.. maybe 2 large ones so I have some left over for the next day. I like having left over pizza to nibble on later. You can make the pizza yourself and bring it to my house or order it for me from a delivery place, but what I'm aiming for is getting food delivered in exchange for bitcoins where I don't have to order or prepare it myself, kind of

like ordering a 'breakfast platter' at a hotel or something, they just bring you something to eat and you're happy!
I like things like onions, peppers, sausage, mushrooms, tomatoes, pepperoni, etc.. just standard stuff no weird fish topping or anything like that. I also like regular cheese pizzas which may be cheaper to prepare or otherwise acquire.

If you're interested please let me know and we can work out a deal.
Thanks,
Laszlo"

On May 22, Laszlo announced that he had successfully exchanged bitcoins with user jercos (Jeremy Sturdivant):

"I just want to report that I successfully traded 10,000 bitcoins for pizza."

Well, that expensive transaction[28] - jercos spent about 40 dollars for two pizzas that in Italy probably would have cost less than 20 euros - turned out to be much more expensive for Laszlo, because today those 10 thousand bitcoins would have a value of around 100 million dollars!
Jercos most likely spent those bitcoins instead of storing them; the final balance of the address he used in October 2018 was 0.00111111 BTC.
He may have transferred them to a cold wallet stored in a secret place but it is definitely more likely that he had used these funds for other transactions at a time when the price of the single bitcoin was significantly lower than the current one.

The fallacy of the reasoning of the supporters of the current monetary system or of its characteristic of adaptive and infinite supply applied also to other systems (even those "crypto-related" like Ethereum), is precisely in considering all the pioneers like savvy investors and savers, with non-human predictive capacities and with a secret communication channel used to communicate each other and guide the market according to their will.

Bitcoin is as fluid and "living" system as the classic one: the difference lies in the tendency to save that a **sound money** like Bitcoin entails, compared to

the tendency to spend promoted by the fiat (**easy money**) system.
For the rest, those who own bitcoins spend, earn, live or survive, like all members of society and therefore, except for rare cases, put his satoshis back into circulation.

FOCUS 2

THE "DANGER" OF BITCOIN DEFLATION

There are those who are frightened by the reduction in monetary inflation, which will become real deflation from around 2140, because historically the periods of inflation close to zero correspond to stagnation of the economy, but there are points to think about:

- **You will not live until 2140.**
- **The reduction in inflation is a problem for the current system,** based on fiat currencies and not on scarce assets.
- **bitcoin is divisible.**

If for the first two points you could provide important arguments such as: "*I will live forever*", "*I worry about my descendants*", "*deflation was a problem even during the Gold Standard*", etc. on the third point I cannot be denied.

1 bitcoin is divisible and its basic unit is satoshi, from the name of its creator. 1 bitcoin = 100 million satoshis.

If we consider what is generally called M0 (Money Supply type 0), ie the set of money that includes all the physical money as metal coins and currencies, deposits and other liquid assets held by central banks[29], and focus on the US Dollar, the most widespread currency on the planet and adopted as a global monetary standard, we discover that the amount of this type of money in circulation is about 1.5 trillion dollars.[30]

They do, in numbers, 1,500,000,000,000,000,000 dollars or 1.5×10^{18} if you prefer to think in terms of power.

On the other hand, the units in Bitcoin, without considering the possibility of splitting them even further, will be a total of 21,000,000 bitcoins or

2,100,000,000,000,000 (2 million and one hundred thousand billion) satoshis or 2.1×10^{15} sats.

In case of need, these units can be divided even more, not going to increase the amount of total value present in the system but further subdividing the units.

An example.

Let's assume that tomorrow the price of the single satoshi is 1 USD.
Since the system currently does not allow smaller units of the satoshi to be moved via blockchain, in this scenario, it would risk not being able to carry out transactions below the single dollar. If we wanted to buy a good for 0.50 USD we could not do it.
Fortunately Bitcoin is digital and in IT it is possible to create "miracles". On blockchain you will not have more than 21 million x 10^8 units of value without a fork, but on a second layer of transmission these limits do not exist: it is already possible to use smaller units using Lightning Network, without touching the Base Protocol.

We will therefore be able to send for example 0.5 satoshis to buy a good with a value of 0.5 USD.

Thanks to this division after the comma, there will be no risk of having a lack of liquidity nor will it be necessary to increase the limit of 21 million bitcoins in circulation.

There will be units of value for all of us.

If we need new units, because the fundamentals will have become too scarce, we could adopt sub-satoshis.
It will therefore be possible to split even more bitcoins without having to touch the basic protocol (BP) but only by acting on the "value unit packages" transferred through the channels on Lightning Network.

The circulation of new units of value will therefore be a fact and will be possible without generating new money from nothing.

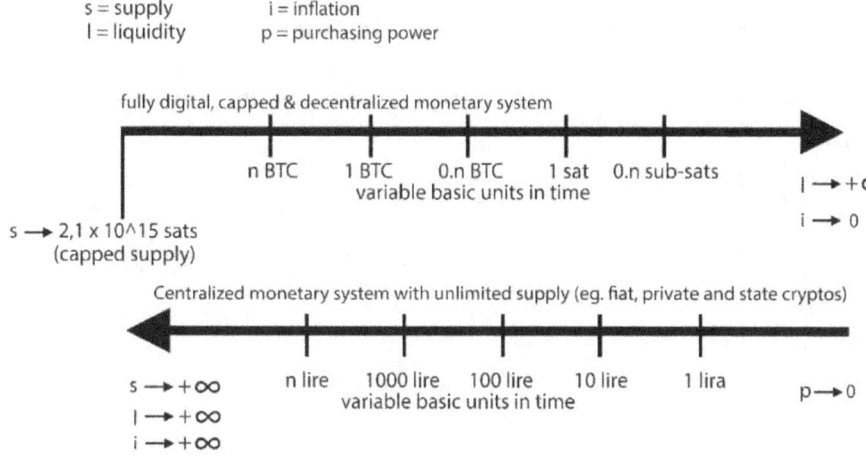

In the picture:

to increase liquidity, new banknotes are entered into the fiat cash system and new denominations are created to compensate for the excess paper available. In the fiat cashless version, new money is printed "out of the thin air" and possibly the base unit is modified to simplify use by the consumer.
Liquidity tends to increase due to the direct influence of the central banking system on monetary policies.
The supply tends to infinity: the higher the monetary inflation (tending to infinity, from the beginning of the system), the greater the supply.
Purchasing power tend to decreases with increasing inflation and therefore with supply.
Deflation is to be avoided.

In the example above, the Italian currency Lira, active from the National Unity of 1861 until 2002.
From an initial base unit of 1 lira, with fractions called cents, we then passed to higher denominations, like the 100 lire coin, and ended up with the 1000 lire banknote, which fell in value until it reached the parity with the Dollar in

1999. Major cuts were necessary to compensate for the increase in the cost of living: the largest banknote was the 500,000 lire. It is customary to think that an increase in the amount of money present in a system also increases the money available to the individual because salaries would also be recalculated.

In reality it is not the case and these graphs, based on the Dollar, show us this.

Growth in productivity and hourly compensation since 1948

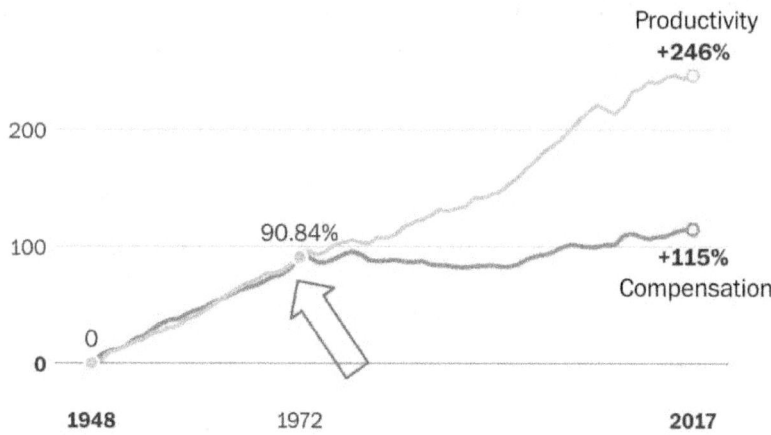

Note: Compensation includes wages and benefits for production and non-supervisory workers

Source: Economic Policy Institute

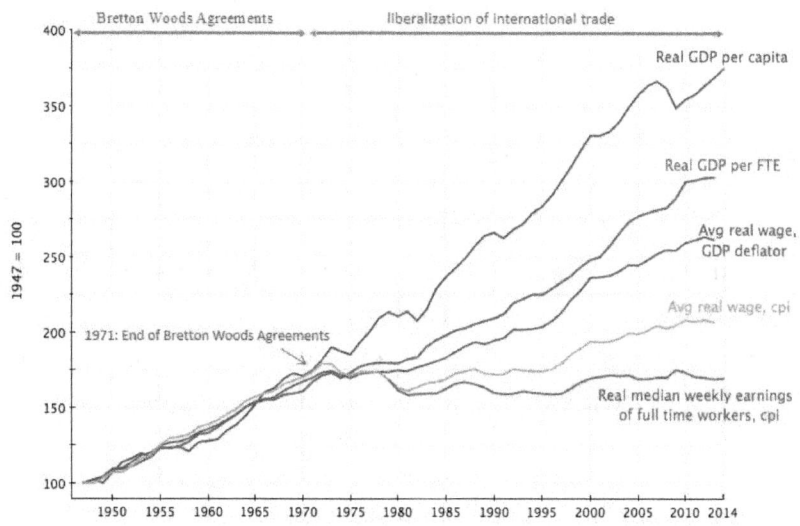

Note: FTE= Full time equivalent worker

Sources: Bureau of Economic Analysis (BEA), Bureau of Labor Statistics (BLS)

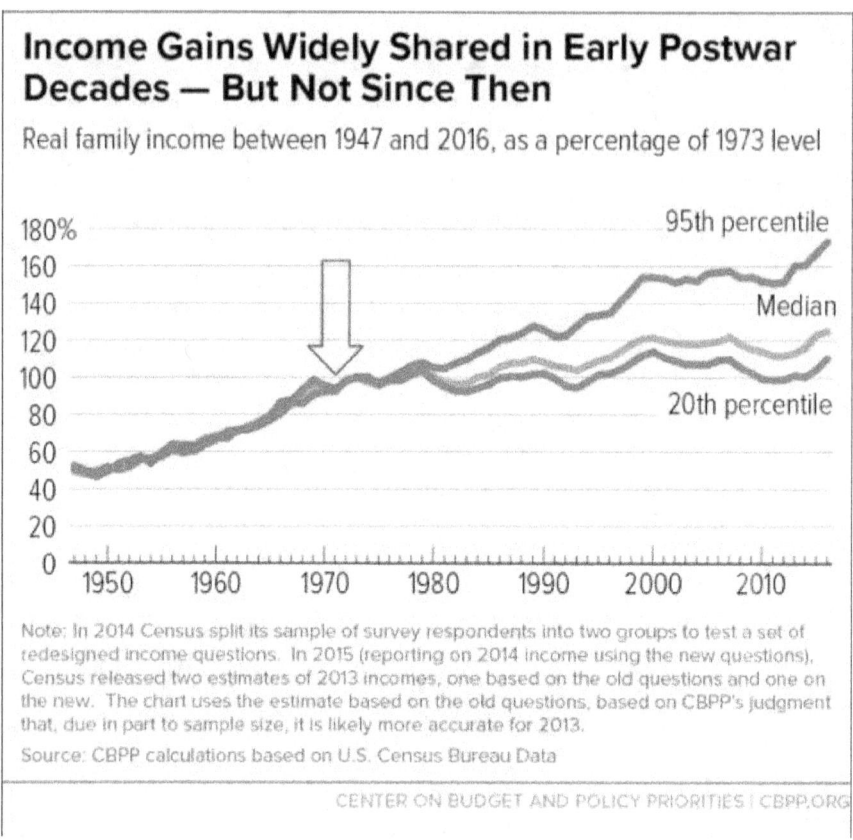

Source: wtfhappenedin1971.com

After the end of the Gold Standard (1971), the increase in productivity and global gross domestic product (RDP, Real gross domestic product) did not correspond to a proportional increase in real wages (adjusted for inflation), whereas previously these indices continued in a linear and proportional manner.

In Bitcoin, in order to increase liquidity you cannot print more currency than the cap (21 million bitcoins) and so expand the supply.

The system is totally digital, therefore, in the absence of liquidity, this can be achieved by splitting.

The base unit is modified downwards to simplify the user's use. Purchasing power increases while monetary inflation tends to zero.

Deflation of the monetary system ceases to be a parameter taken into consideration.

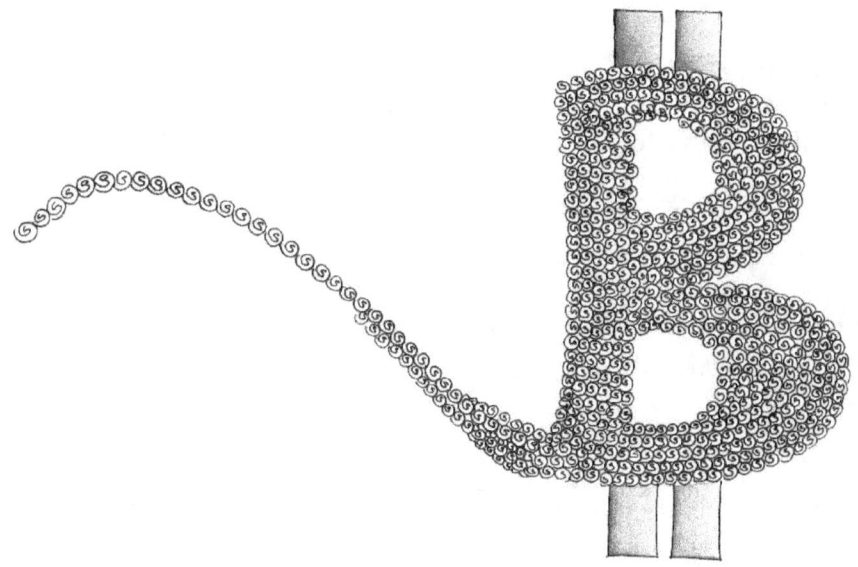

QUESTION 22

WHY SHOULD I CONVERT MY SAVINGS INTO SOMETHING SO VOLATILE?

You should not.

But I take advantage of this question to elaborate a more articulated speech.

Some people ask me: "*should I buy bitcoin?*" Or: "*is it a good time to buy?*" My first answer is: "*I am a tech guy, not a financial advisor*".

If they insist, the answer is: "*it's never a good time to buy bitcoin, but it's always a good time to buy bitcoins!*".

I explain below the meaning of this apparently meaningless phrase.

It's never a good time if you don't know what it is, how it works and why it works. Simply put, don't buy what you don't know. It applies to everything: your money is precious.

Do not be advised by anyone, think with your head and VERIFY.

It's always a good time to buy bitcoins if, after studying a bit, you want to buy fractions of bitcoins - as we have seen, the real basic value unit of the system is the satoshi (sat) - because you have realized that your current money is not as valuable as you thought: never buy everything at once and in periods of growth in value, but rather buy a little at a time (eg the value of a pack of cigarettes a week) possibly in periods of decline, regardless of current value of the single bitcoin.

What if the Bitcoin experiment fails?
You will lose the investment!
Therefore never spend what you are not willing to lose.

Are you willing to invest your hard-earned savings on what is today a bet on the future? Not me.
If instead you want to spend a pack of cigarettes a week, if you are a smoker it is also healthy!

However, the initial question allows us to analyze the concept of volatility a little bit.

Far be it from me to dwell on concepts proper to an economic text - *Saifedean Ammous's The Bitcoin Standard* is certainly more useful in this sense - let's see briefly why Bitcoin's volatility is not necessarily bad.

When we are dealing with a volatile asset we are led to believe that its price always goes in the wrong direction and that it does so from when we bought it: if we buy today, this asset will surely lose value starting from tomorrow, so it's not worth buying.
As if the direction taken by the curve on the graph depended on us.
In fact it can also be partly true.

If we buy a highly speculative asset and we do it at a time of hype, ie market excitement (**FOMO**), we will contribute to the creation of the speculative bubble and we will almost certainly suffer the consequences, which, in finance, are the ruinous fall in the price followed by periods of decline (**Bear**

market) and liquidation at a loss, because the typical reasoning of those who improvise "traders" is: "*if the value has fallen, it will fall again, so it is better to go out at a loss and recover a little something*".

Tell the truth: you find yourself with what was said above, right?

It almost always happens when you approach Bitcoin from a speculative point of view, before moving on to the study of technology.

In Bitcoin, you pay for volatility, but you do it only when you exit the investment to limit your losses.

This volatility, however, can also be ridden if, as we have said before, we buy few satoshis at a time and with constancy, regardless of the price of the single bitcoin.

If we go to *dcabtc.com* and set a weekly investment of 5 dollars, for example, we can see how many sats we would have accumulated in a variable period and how much we would have exploited the volatility in the exchange with the Dollar.

We make things more interesting.

In 2017 there was the big Bitcoin bubble, which brought the price of the single BTC from around 1,000 usd in April, to 18.700 in December, before breaking out ruinously, until the value of the single bitcoin reached 3,500 USD in February 2019.

Even now, when I talk about Bitcoin, there is always someone who says: "*I -* or a friend of mine, or an acquaintance ... the subject changes from time to time - *I lost a lot of money with that Bitcoin*!".

Well, let's use dcabtc.com again and see how this bubble could be ridden without loss.
We set an investment of 5 USD weekly, the accumulation for two years and the start two years ago (from August 2017 to August 2019).

Although we had begun to invest in full bubble, today we would have around 8 million satoshis and an increase in value in USD of about 35% compared to what we invested.

We would have spent a total of 500 dollars and now we would have had 700 USD, despite the fact that the current bitcoin price is 10,000 USD (August 2019) while in December 2017 we bought for 18,000 dollars.

What if we had limited the investment to just one year?

Well, we would have lost about 10% of our investment, rather than 40% we would have lost if we had invested everything while bitcoin was worth 18,000 USD.

This investment strategy is called **Dollar Cost Averaging*** and consists of investing a certain amount of money on a regular basis rather than at the same time.

In this way we minimize the risk by removing a variable, namely short-term volatility, and the emotional element, because we are no longer forced to monitor the price of the single bitcoin while waiting to find the right time to invest.

*The information shown above does not constitute a financial advisory service in any way. The proposed analyzes cannot in any way replace the free and informed judgment of the investor, which always and exclusively acts at his own risk.

QUESTION 23

HOW MUCH DOES IT COST TO BUY BITCOINS?

The bitcoins, or better, the satoshis, represent monetary units and as such can be bought and/or sold as other monetary units.

When we have to travel abroad and the destination country does not use our currency, we must necessarily change money.

This change usually takes place in two ways: either by going to a currency exchange (a shop, a bank counter, an app) or between individuals.

A very trivial example: if I go to Albania I know that the local currency is the Lek. I will therefore have to go to a currency exchange to sell my euros and buy leks, or I'll have to exchange some banknotes in my currency for a certain number of cash in lek with some local person, based on a conventional exchange rate (for eg 1 euro for 120 lek).

The same concept applies to Bitcoin as well.

If I want to buy bitcoins I will have to sell euros, while if I want to sell them I will have to buy euros (or other fiat currency), and I will be able to do so on special sites called exchange or through ATMs, or directly between private individuals.

Buying bitcoins therefore does not have a fixed cost, because it is based on a conventional exchange, for example the current price on Kraken or on Coinmarketcap, but may have commissions, especially if we buy from ATMs.

These commissions, or fees, range on average from 0.25% to 10% and are applied by those who sell us bitcoins or euros.

The average commission paid at a local currency exchange (ATM) is 10%; it can be deduced that, at a cost of 100 euros, I will get satoshis for a value of 90 euros.

Be careful also at what price is shown during the exchange phase!

If in the ATM the price of a whole bitcoin is 10,000 euros but we know that at the moment it is sold on average at 9,500 euros, then we are in the presence of another commission, this time a hidden one.

Taking the example again: if we sell 100 euros at this ATM we will get 0.009 bitcoins or 0.01 bitcoins minus 10% commission. In satoshi there are 900,000 sats (ie 1 million satoshis minus 10%).

If the exchange rate had been based on the average price, we would have obtained about 0.00947368 bitcoins, or 0.01052632 bitcoins minus 10%. In satoshi they are 947,368 sats.

On 100 euros the ATM has held 10 euros of commissions plus about 5 euros of "hidden" fees.

It may seem little, but on 1,000 euros they start to become important commissions.

Moreover, if a person thinks in satoshi and considers the potential increase in value per unit as the years go by, 47 thousand less satoshis are not few!

It is up to us to choose the most convenient exchange rate, just as we would do when we have to change euros for dollars or, taking my example, euros for lek or other local currency.

QUESTION 24

WHY SHOULDN'T I KEEP MY BITCOINS ON AN EXCHANGE?

We can buy bitcoins (or satoshis) even on an online exchange but we should never keep our funds firm on it.

The reason is quite simple: we do not have the private key of our wallet on the exchange, since this provides us with a custodial wallet. Imagine that you want to convert euros into dollars: would you trust to leave your money at the local exchange after converting them?

To better understand the dangers of not having your own funds directly using the private key, I invite you to read the chapter *Has anyone ever stolen bitcoins from the system?*

So let's use the exchange for the purchase of satoshis and the temporary maintenance of them, if we wanted to use it to do trading activities, but remember that it does NOT provide a non-custodial wallet!

QUESTION 25

WHY IS DIGITAL GOLD BETTER THAN MATERIAL GOLD?

Often bitcoin, as a monetary unit, is called "**digital gold**".

The reason for this definition is mainly linked to two characteristics shared by bitcoin and gold: **it is a scarce commodity and it is difficult to produce.**

It has nothing to do with the cost of a single bitcoin or the value attributed to the Bitcoin Protocol!
If tomorrow the single bitcoin should cost 100 euros instead of 10,000, the two properties shown above would continue to be valid.

Gold is currently a better **Store of Value** (SoV), simply because it has had more time to consolidate its market position.

At a theoretical level Bitcoin should also over time constitute a reserve of value and therefore allow the user to maintain his purchasing power or even increase it.

However, Bitcoin has features that make it better than gold as a medium of exchange.

Let's see them together.

Main features	GOLD SYSTEM	BITCOIN SYSTEM
FUNGIBILITY	High fungibility with gold Low fungibility with digital gold tokens, subject to seizure	Medium fungibility on blockchain High fungibility with satoshi on second layers
DURABILITY	High durability	Private key can be lost. Digital cash is unseizable, unhackable, undestroyable
PORTABILITY	Good for medium trades bad for big trades	Excellent portability Digital only
DIVISIBILITY	Good divisibility	Excellent divisibility
SECURITY	Exposure to counterfeit Funds management personal or by a third party	Granted by decentralization and PoW Not your keys, not your BTC
COUNTERFEIT	Counterfeiting affects certified marks	Impossible to counterfeit a private key
EASY TO TRANSACT	High amount transactions are expensive and complex	P2P Transactions Can be expensive on blockchain, cheap or free on second layers
SCARCITY	Good scarcity (now) but unpredictable supply	Predictable circulating and total supply

FUNGIBILITY: we have previously said that this term indicates an asset that can be exchanged for another of equal attributed value.

For example, we can exchange one 10k gold coin with another that has the same chemical/physical characteristics.

In the digital environment it is difficult to guarantee fungibility in a context in which a third party can intervene and cancel transactions or seize money. My money could be dirty and therefore not as good as yours.

Bitcoin tries to solve this problem by introducing the concept of irreversibility of transactions and excluding the third part.

The level of fungibility of the unmarked gold is higher than that of Bitcoin if we consider the bitcoin exchanges on the base layer (via blockchain), while it is comparable if we consider the exchanges on Lightning Network.

DURABILITY: gold like bitcoin is not perishable, an excellent feature if you want to use these goods as money.

PORTABILITY: gold portability is good if we consider small businesses (eg buying a car), it is very bad considering big businesses.
Bitcoin portability is excellent and does not rely on the medium used (just an app on the phone).

DIVISIBILITY: both assets are divisible but Bitcoin is more suited to micropayments (on Lightning Network). Bitcoin is divisible up to 8 decimal places for blockchain transactions, while it is up to sub-satoshi figures for those on Lightning Network. This ease in splitting is possible because the bitcoin asset is completely digital.

SECURITY: Bitcoin security is given by its decentralization and the computing power used by miners to support the network (hashrate). The greater this calculation power and the number of miners, the lower the chance that transactions will be rewritten or made reversible.
Currently (August 2019) the cost for an attack on the Bitcoin network is estimated by Messari (messari.io) at around $ 160,000,000 a day, with an attacker who is able to directly collect and manage more than 50% of the system's computing power.
The network is therefore considered relatively safe, given the impossibility for an attacker to coordinate a similar attack and the system's tendency to increase total hashrate, currently close to 100 million TH/s.

#	Asset	Price USD	Liquid Marketcap	%down from ATH	Attack Cost / day
1	Bitcoin . BTC	$10,240.76	$183,647,997,296	49%	$162,802,381
4	Bitcoin Cash . BCH	$295.64	$5,326,442,366	93%	$4,196,731
2	Ethereum . ETH	$178.68	$19,165,401,626	88%	$3,586,672
9	Bitcoin SV . BSV	$116.75	$2,100,965,575	54%	$1,948,947
29	Dogecoin . DOGE	$0.00240	$287,236,259	87%	$578,826
5	Litecoin . LTC	$67.65	$4,284,772,485	82%	$561,758
28	Zcash . ZEC	$44.01	$326,274,841	95%	$559,630
16	Dash . DASH	$91.27	$824,522,444	94%	$516,817
42	Ravencoin . RVN	$0.0306	$134,970,693	61%	$297,823
17	Ethereum Classic . ETC	$6.13	$697,242,443	87%	$239,321

Individual security is instead given by the ability of users to secure their private keys (see "*Has anyone ever stolen bitcoins from the system?*"). On the other hand, the security of gold is given by factors such as:

- exposure to counterfeiting
- management of funds by individuals
- management of funds by a third party
- susceptibility to seizures by the State or other legal entity

Counterfeiting is a problem that also affects institutions that store and manage funds; if it is true that a counterfeit of minerals can be easily discovered, it is also true that it is possible that the marks stamped on the gold bars may be counterfeit.

Recently it was discovered that counterfeit gold bars were stored in the vaults of JP Morgan Chase & Co for a value of 50 million euros. The fakes are sophisticated, so other thousands of fake gold bars may not have been identified yet.[31]

The fakes are real gold. The marks on the bars are counterfeit.

This counterfeit is a relatively new way of breaking global measures taken to block "conflict minerals", that is, coming from conflict zones and sold primarily to perpetuate wars, and to prevent money laundering.

Consequently, we move on to the fourth factor listed above, namely the susceptibility to seizures by the State, minor in Bitcoin thanks to the pseudo-anonymity of the system itself.

The management of gold funds, especially for high sums of money, takes place on behalf of reliable third parties: typically banks subject to regulations. As for Bitcoin, this can be done in total autonomy, even for large amounts. For minor amounts, gold can be relatively simple to store but more subject to the risk of theft or extortion than Bitcoin: it is undoubtedly easier to keep a sheet containing a private key, or even memorize it, than to store and secure 1 Kg of gold.

The management of the funds by a third party involves a centralization of the resources that exposes to the dangers expressed in the chapter *Why was Bitcoin created?*, in particular if the management system of the institution is centralized and the gold is "tokenized", ie represented by a digital token issued by the institution.

EASY TO TRANSACT: transactions in gold for high amounts are expensive and complex. They require intensive coordination and very high commissions, unless the assets are tokenized.
Bitcoin transactions are almost immediate (hours for Bitcoin on blockchain, days/weeks/months for physical gold) and can be realized directly between the two parties that want to exchange value.

SCARCITY: both assets are scarce but the amount of units of value in the Bitcoin system is totally predictable (**predictable supply**), while it is not for gold.
The discovery of a large gold deposit could lead to a shock to the global market with a consequent reduction in the role of gold as a Store of Value, to the point of reducing its use solely for secondary purposes (eg computer industry, technology, furniture). These are not remote hypotheses: with the reinforcement of the space industry it will be possible to search for precious metal deposits on relatively close celestial bodies and take it.
Bitcoin was created with the express purpose of acting as a monetary unit and could potentially replace gold as a global Store of Value.

QUESTION 26

WHAT IS LIGHTNING NETWORK?

Lightning Network (LNP) is a structure of **payment channels** open between private individuals and/or companies and represents the scaling solution for Bitcoin; that's why we often called it also the Bitcoin' Second Layer.

With Lightning we can potentially make hundreds of thousands if not million transactions for second and so reach any part of the World (almost) instantaneously.

"Yes, and for free!"

Not really.

We can transact on Lightning Network and we can do it for a really cheap fee per transaction: personally I never spent more then 10 sats in fees.

But this will not be the case for so long.

Before exploring why and what we can do, let's see a bit how Lightning Network works.

Each member of the network can create his own node, equipped with a wallet, in which he can keep a certain amount of satoshis, or he can rely on a custodial service, with all the criticalities that ensue.

When an user wants to send a payment to another person or service on the network, he can open a communication channel with it, within which the satoshis will travel, just as the data packets routed by the transport protocols, such as TCP, travel between the devices connected to the Internet. The discussion on the structure underlying the Internet is a bit complicated so we will go into it later.

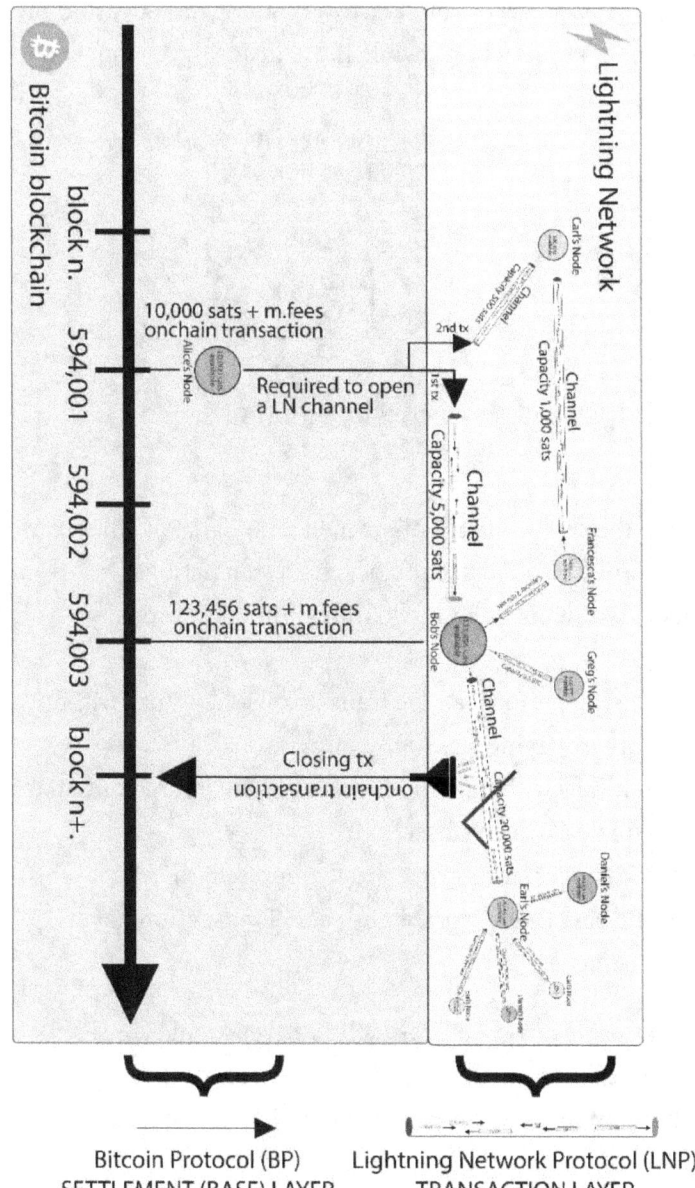

In the image on the previous page: the black arrows coming directly from the nodes represent blockchain transactions, while those inside the channel are Lightning transactions.

By convention, only three transactions are shown as directly related to the Bitcoin blockchain and are used to open two channels, Alice's with Bob and Alice's with Carl, and to close the channel that Bob opened with Earl. All other black arrows outside the channels also represent blockchain transactions.

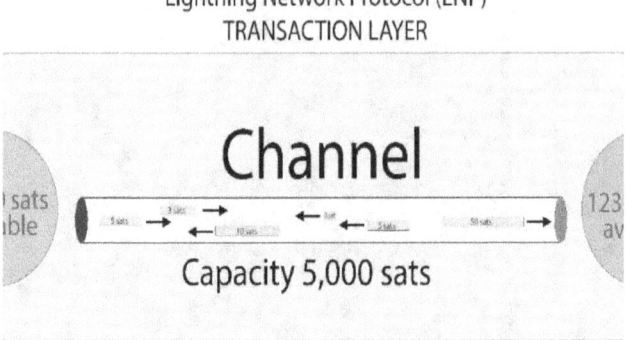

Alice was able to open two channels with two different nodes through two onchain transactions.
Within the channels she can perform all the transactions she wants, without waiting for confirmations or paying fees to the miners.
Bob closes the channel he has with Earl and his satoshis are poured onto the blockchain through a single closing transaction.
In the first image the two large panels symbolically represent the two layers: **Settlement Layer**, as the base layer (blockchain), and **Transaction Layer** (Lightning Network channels).

The representation of the most correct Transaction Layer should consider only the payment channels and not the transactions outside of them, but for reasons related to the simplification of the representation on levels, this solution has been chosen.

Let's make it easy. How it works with an example.

Imagine that you are in a group of five friends with a fixed appointment: friday night at the pub.
Every time you go and drink and eat together, you go to the pub checkout

and have your bill split so that everyone pays for what they have consumed. The owner of the pub will have to print more receipts, spend some time to collect the money from the individuals by increasing the line in front of the cashier, and be careful to reach the correct total. In short, this system is inefficient; it's slow, expensive, definitely not scalable.

Now let's assume that you and your friends want to do things more efficiently.

You calculate that each month you spend an average of 100 satoshis each. You could put these 100 satoshis in a common fund and keep each of you the bill on the expenses made.
Once you reach the pub checkout you can pay the owner in a lump sum, knowing that none of you will lose out because you know exactly how much the individuals spent.
From the following month, if Alice, a member of the group, spent 50 satoshis, she will integrate the common fund with 50 satoshis, if Bob has spent 20, he will add the same number to reach the 100 satoshis, and so on.

The common fund could also be useful outside the pub: if Bob wants to buy a pizza that costs 5 satoshis but has no money with him, he could ask for a loan from the common fund he has with his friends and integrate 5 satoshis at the next expense at the pub.
On a pub bill of 20 satoshis each, Bob will pay 24 and all the others 19.

These extra expenses can take place a theoretically infinite number of times, the important thing is that each member of the group keeps track of the expenses and that each month everyone has a balance of 100 satoshis.

This is similar to what happens with the Bitcoin second layer called Lightning Network.[32]

You and your four friends open a payment channel (in the example, the common fund) by executing a single transaction each on the Bitcoin blockchain. Instead of being a standard transaction, which requires a single signature to spend the funds, this is a **multi-signature** transaction. Multi-signature transactions are, in a nutshell, complex and programmable transactions, which allow different parties to participate. Individuals cannot perform outward transactions without the authorization (signatures) of the other participants.

The parties are anchored to the Bitcoin blockchain by a multi-signature contract and can now send transactions between them within the channel, without the need to transmit all to the blockchain. The channel requires funds to be inserted inside it: **it is necessary that at least one of the parties involved in the opening of the channel pay the funds.**

This money inserted in the payment channel is called **Channel Capacity**, that is the satoshis capacity of the channel just opened.

Channel participants keep track of the balance (**channel states**) and only send the last balance of the channel to the Bitcoin blockchain if they wish to close the latter.

So if Bob wants to get out of the common fund, he can do it: his debt to the fund will be calculated and he can take the satoshis left out of Lightning Network, back to the blockchain, minus the usual mining fee for the onchain transaction.

A true P2P electronic cash system

So now we understand that **Lightning Network is a structure of payment channels where users can exchange satoshis directly with each other, without a miner collecting their transactions and inserting them in a new block.**

The only mining fees you and your friends will have to pay will be those of sending satoshis to a Lightning node for opening a payment channel with it and those for closing the channel with consequent sending of the remaining satoshis to the Bitcoin blockchain, instead of all those deriving from the individual onchain transactions that you would usually do.

For each channel that you want to open a channel capacity is established: let's say that I have 0.01 BTC in my wallet, or 1 million satoshis. I could decide to open a direct channel with a friend of mine with a capacity of 20,000 satoshis, one of 100,000 satoshis with my favorite pub and many others. I will then be able to execute all the transactions I want using these channels without having to close them. The pub, on the other hand, may from time to time decide to transfer satoshis to its onchain cold wallet, just to keep important quantities offline and protected thanks to the (tendency to) immutability of the Bitcoin blockchain.

Not just direct channels

If Lightning Network would allow the transfer of satoshis only to direct channels it would be completely useless, or better, its usefulness would be only for recurring payments between two people and/or companies in direct contact. In reality this network allows to have what in jargon is called **Payment Routing**: I can send satoshis even to those who are not directly connected to me through "jumps", called hops, between nodes.

Imagine that a friend has to pay for his beer at the pub but does not have a direct payment channel with the place.
Instead of opening one, with the resulting fees to be paid and waiting time, because it would have to wait for confirmations of the onchain transaction, this reads the pub's invoice and pays: the satoshis will first pass by a channel opened by our friend with another person and will jump from node to node until they reach someone whose node has a direct channel with the pub.

In our example, if our friend has a direct channel with our node and we have one with the pub, it could happen that the satoshis will pass by our node first and then arrive at the pub's node.

The more nodes available to the Lightning Network, the easier it is to make these indirect payments. Few nodes mean a high possibility that the payment is not successful!

It is as if, in the material world, we had to pay a person who is in another city using banknotes: we can hand over the money to one of our acquaintances and this will deliver it to other people, until it reaches the real recipient. Obviously, although similar to an indirect payment system of the material world, here there is no danger that one of the participants in charge of delivering the money to the next will run off with the loot, because the network is based on **smart contracts** and not on direct intervention of people.

Lightning therefore constitutes a true P2P network, in full compliance with the abstract of the Bitcoin whitepaper created by Satoshi Nakamoto, while the Base (Settlement) Layer, with its blockchain, is more similar to a broadcast system, since the transaction transcription and so their irreversibility depends on the miners.

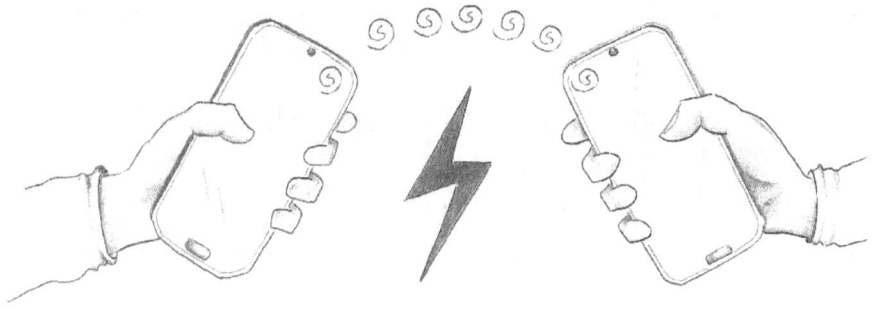

The Lightning Network Fee Market

Every transaction comes with a price. This is true for any kind of transaction, and if in the classic transaction layers (for example Visa or Mastercard) you don't pay fees, it's because someone is paying them for you: usually the store owner, that, if it's smart, will increase a little bit the price of its goods to cover the commissions.

This is also true for Lightning Network.

"Ok, but how much I need to pay?"

It depends.

If with Bitcoin onchain transactions you pay a mining fee that correspond to the fees you want to pay multiplied by the size in byte of your transaction — you could potentially pay high fees for a transaction with low economic value and low fees for a high value TX (see Appendix IV, *"How much does it cost to send bitcoins?"*)— , with Lighting you could have literally ZERO fees but you have other parameters to consider.

Base Fee: when you open a channel with a node, you should know what's the Base Fee it will require for every transaction that goes through it and reach another node.
If the Base Fee is for example 1 sat, you will pay 1 sat as a fixed price.

Fee Rate: when you send a transaction, this go through a node and this has set a Fee Rate, you pay a percentage of the total amount as a fee.
Fee Rate is expressed in mili mSats, so for example if a node ask for 1000 mili mSats as a Fee Rate, it will ask for 0.001 sats.
You need to multiply this amount for your total amount.

You want to transfer 2000 sats? you pay 1 sat (Base Fee) + 2000 x 0.001 sats (Fee Rate) = 3 sats as a fee (Base Fee + Fee Rate).

Is that all?

No.

You need also to consider the amount of hops your transaction will need to do!

If you don't have a direct channel with a node and you need to pay for a service, you will relay on another node and it will eventually do the same with another one, until the service's node is reached. We saw that before and we call it Payment Routing.

So, let's say Alice need to pay David — yes, more sats for me! — but doesn't have a direct channel with him.

Alice has a direct channel with Bob, Bob has a channel with Carol and Carol with David.

The transaction will need to go through 2 nodes!

So, let's say these node have the same Fee Rate and Base Fee: Alice needs to pay Carol too, not only Bob, so 2x the fees.

Now the 2000 sats for David will need 6 sats to go through.

As you can see, even if the fees are low (0.3% of the total amount), they are not zero.

It's important to note that Alice can decide the max amount of fees she is willing to pay.

If 6 sats are too high for her, she could select a smaller cap: let's say 3 sats.

Her node will calculate another route to David (if any) in which routing nodes require less fee.

Alice and David are both connected to Isaac, an LSP (Lightning Service Provider). This has a Fee Rate of 1000 mili mSats and a Base Fee of zero sats.

If Alice pays David 2000 sats, she will need to pay only 2000 x 0.001 sats (Fee Rate) = 2 sats.

She will pay the 0.1% of the total amount as a fee.

So, as you can see, if a user set a max amount of fee that he/she is willing to pay, the node will search for the best route with the lowest fee.

The Lightning Network Fee Market is starting

We can understand that node operators have two main options:

1. They could decide to keep the fee almost static and even high if compared to the average, in order to keep their channel balanced and sporadically earn some high routing fees.
2. They could follow (or better, create) the market and have dynamic fees so they can have more routing events, earn less per routing but have an overall bigger routing fees adding up all the transactions.

What can we do to be active users and to keep the fees low?

Well, first of all we should start creating node and opening channels.

It's better to have many nodes that a lot of channels with a small network of nodes!

Then, we should select good nodes in terms of capacity and availability, but we can also look at the Base Fee and Fee rate required.

In my case, I created a sort of price list for my routing services:

So it's like I'm selling my route service (or capacity) for a price: in this case I request zero sats as Base Fee and a variable Fee Rate that start from 1 mili mSat (0.000001 sats) and reach 2000 mili mSat (0.002 sat) if a user open a channel with 2 million sats of capacity to my node.

This price list will eventually change, adapting to the Lightning Network Fee Market, once the network will be bigger and there will be more competition between routing nodes.

Just in case you want to open a channel to my node, now you know my prices and here is my QR Code URI:

QUESTION 27

What is a Sidechain?

A sidechain is an alternative chain of blocks to the Bitcoin blockchain and constitutes an external solution of scalability.

This chain contains tokens that represent a certain amount of bitcoins: when you want to use it, you sends a certain quantity of BTC to a smart contract that will keep them locked and allow you to carry out some transactions with these tokens. If the user wishes to exit the sidechain he will be able to get his bitcoins again by returning the tokens to the address specified by the smart contract.

Bitcoin's most famous sidechain is currently **Blockstream's Liquid Network**.

The sidechain solutions are not comparable to the Bitcoin blockchain from a decentralization the point of view. These networks are in the hands of federations, in which the number of nodes is limited in order to guarantee a higher speed of transaction execution.

When considering the use of sidechain it is mainly done to take advantage of features not present in the Bitcoin blockchain or to have faster and more privacy-oriented transactions.
However, trust comes into play: we must trust that the various members of the federation retain a reserve of 100% of the assets represented by their tokens and that these nodes are in sufficient numbers not to be easily attacked from the outside, guaranteeing that the network is not disabled.

QUESTION 28

WAS BITCOIN INVENTED BY THE AMERICAN NSA (NATIONAL SECURITY AGENCY)?

We do not know the true identity of Satoshi Nakamoto. We don't even know if a single person or a group of researchers and developers was hiding under this pseudonym.

So where does this belief that the NSA could be behind the development of Bitcoin come from?

We find the first clue in the hash algorithm used in Bitcoin: the SHA256.

SHA is a term that designates a family of cryptographic hash functions invented by the NSA, in which we also find the SHA256.

But then if the NSA invented these cryptographic functions and if this agency is known for its espionage even on private citizens, surely there must be some sinister in Bitcoin!

Let's start by saying that many of the technologies we use today have actually been the subject of research by state or parastatal agencies.

An example of this is the Internet, derived from Arpanet, an interconnection network created in 1969 by the Defense of the United States.

And yet we use the Internet, and we can also do it by fighting the censorship imposed by states. Why?

The concept of open source, already analyzed previously, returns.

These are open technologies, realized by actors who could exploit them for anti-ethical purposes but usable by everyone and, above all, analysable.

134

Returning to the SHA256 it must therefore be said that it is an open standard and that over the years it has been analyzed by hundreds of thousands of researchers and developers.

It therefore becomes unlikely that the NSA has inserted a backdoor in the code and that this has not yet been identified.

In addition to the technical reasons that led to the belief, by someone, that the NSA may be behind the development of Bitcoin, there are also documents that, if poorly analyzed, can lead to certain conclusions.

One above all is HOW TO MAKE A MINT: THE CRYPTOGRAPHY OF ANONYMOUS ELECTRONIC CASH by Laurie Law, Susan Sabett, Jerry Solinas.[33]

This is not a whitepaper describing a technology proposed or created by the authors of the document, but it's an interesting study by the NSA on existing technologies, in particular on the critical issues of the cashless monetary system and the tradeoffs of the new electronic cash system.

NSA inventions are not illustrated.

The blind signatures system invented by David Chaum, then applied in eCash, is analyzed, but above all the term Electronic Cash is well described which, as in Bitcoin, indicates the portability of the concept of material cash in the digital world, with all due respect of those who still believe that cash means only "spendable money" and therefore oppose it to the concept of Store of Value.

With hindsight it's interesting to see that there was not so much to get to Bitcoin and that the tradeoffs and the criticalities illustrated here could be solved with the "simple" decentralization of the system.

QUESTION 29

IS IT TRUE THAT CRIMINALS USE BITCOIN?

Of course!

Criminals use Bitcoin as they use other technologies such as the Internet, smartphones, computers, cars, etc.
I will say more: it seems absurd but criminals, as the first medium of exchange, use the Dollar!

Out of irony, the objection raised by some about the use that criminals can make of Bitcoin is at least ridiculous.
People use Bitcoin for the most diverse purchases: homes, cars, technology, drugs, illegal material.
In short, it is a medium of exchange and it is used like the others.
So it's foolish to worry about the uses you make of money. On the contrary, we would have to worry if the money we use proves to be conditioned by a central authority, somehow castrated and therefore no longer neutral.

Andreas M. Antonopoulos, professor and author of books on Bitcoin, such as eg. *Mastering Bitcoin* and *The Internet of Money*, it is usual to explain this association between Bitcoin and "forbidden" purchases in this way:
"People ask me, aren't you worried about the fact that you can buy drugs with this money (bitcoin)?
As far as I concern I don't know any form of money you can't buy drugs with.

More specifically, drugs are the second most traded commodity after food in the world, and have been such in the last one hundred and fifty thousand years. If you couldn't buy drugs with your money, I would argue it's not actually money.

So one of the criteria of money is that you can purchase products and services and if you can't purchase the second most traded commodity in the world with it, then it's not real money."

I don't think there is a better answer.

Furthermore, a great debate could be opened about what is illegal and what is not.

In a global context, for example, can cannabis purchase be defined "illegal"?

Definitely no.

In fact, there are states in which the purchase of cannabinoids and opioids is totally legal, others in which it is restricted and others in which it is absolutely forbidden, with penalties ranging from simple fine to, unfortunately, death.
Think, in some countries it is illegal to even buy alcohol, while in Europe the ban is only for minors, in other it is even illegal to buy some literary genres!

In short, Bitcoin is an excellent payment system also and above all for the fact of being neutral, not conditioned by the policy of those who use bitcoins or who controls large capitals.
The same cannot be said about the digital Dollar (or Euro).

QUESTION 30

HAS ANYONE EVER STOLEN BITCOINS FROM THE SYSTEM?

No.

It is not possible, due to the technology and the encryption algorithms used, to steal bitcoins from the system.

You cannot crack a private key and appropriate the funds.

From a definition provided by Bellaj Badr, CTO and founder of Mchain: "A Bitcoin private key (ECC key) is an integer between one and about 10^{77}. This may not seem like much of a selection, but for practical purposes it's essentially infinite. If you could process one trillion private keys per second, it would take more than one million times the age of the universe to count them all. Even worse, just enumerating these keys would consume more than the total energy output of the sun for 32 years. This vast keyspace plays a fundamental role in securing the Bitcoin network."[34]

It's different if, instead, we consider the theft of bitcoins to the users or the loss of the private keys.

According to a ranking provided by Airbitz Inc., the largest threats to user funds are, in order of statistical significance:[35]

1. User error (lost devices, lost backups, etc.)
2. Social engineering (phishing, SIM port, etc.)
3. Third Party Custodial Risk (exchange or bank hack, fraud)
4. Malware (keyloggers, screen captures)
5 Physical attack (wrench/gun/knife attack)

As mentioned above, if we use an app that does not allow us to backup our private keys and lose our device, we have lost funds. Therefore always use applications that allow you to transcribe private keys.

It goes without saying that if we lose our paper wallet containing the private keys backup we are screwed again. User error is, as in many other areas, in the first place among the causes of loss of funds.

The second cause is the attack by other people using so-called social engineering, which is realized in particular through phishing.

Phishing is a type of online scam that involves trying to get the victim to release sensitive data, in this case access to our electronic wallet.

This scam takes place mainly through communication channels such as e-mail and messaging (Telegram, WhatsApp): the attacker usually sends the link to a seemingly reliable site and asks to enter private keys, or even directly asks the user for them.

Custody of funds with third parties typically occurs when the user leaves his bitcoins on an exchange which, being a centralized system, is exposed to all the risks inherent in such a system: hacking, DDoS attacks, technical downtimes, etc.
There are many cases of violated exchange and deprived of user funds. The most striking case is certainly that of MtGox, an exchange with a troubled history of investigations, hacking and bankruptcies. Because of the hacker attacks, the company lost around 850,000 bitcoins, which when compared to today's value of bitcoins in USD make over 8 billion dollars.

The last major attack to an exchange occurred in May 2019 against Binance. 7000 bitcoins were stolen in a single transaction without the exchange realizing it!

The press tends, intentionally or by simple ignorance, to associate these attacks and these losses with an alleged lack of security of the Bitcoin network. This is absolutely false because, as we have said, exchanges, centralized systems exposed to the same identical risks as credit institutions, or users, not the Bitcoin network, were and still are attacked.

For all the situations described above, the following applies: "**not your keys, not your bitcoins**".

The user who approaches Bitcoin needs to understand that the funds are managed entirely by him and not by a third party. We are our bank and we must secure our money.

There is very little to say about physical attack: always protect yourself and your loved ones, even before your money. The only suggestion I can give you is to use a lark mirror: leave few funds on a paper wallet and put it in a place that is easily accessible.
If criminals ever force you to give them your bitcoins, you can give this paper wallet, knowing you haven't lost your entire capital.

QUESTION 31

WHAT DOES BITCOIN MAXIMALIST MEAN?

"Bitcoin maximalist" term was born as a mockery from supporters of alternative cryptocurrencies against those who until then were simply called bitcoiners.

Vitalik Buterin, creator of Ethereum, in his article called "*On Bitcoin Maximalism, and Currency and Platform Network Effects*" - I suggest reading it because it is very interesting - began by describing Bitcoin maximalism as: "*the idea that an environment of multiple competing cryptocurrencies is undesirable, that it is wrong to launch "yet another coin", and that it is both righteous and inevitable that the Bitcoin currency comes to take a monopoly position in the cryptocurrency scene.*[36]"

As I said, the article is very interesting but Vitalik, a genious without any doubt, insists on this overlap between the bitcoin currency and the protocol, generating confusion, it is not known whether deliberately or unconsciously. He even describes the maximalist bitcoiner as one who sees positively the monopoly of an asset within a free market.

Well, from that article on, many bitcoiners started playing and defining themselves as maximalists, not because they found themselves in the description provided by Vitalik, but because they basically didn't recognize the need for different infrastructures, above all Ethereum, on which to build their libertarian dream.

But you know, the joke's gone far enough!

Here new maximalists arrived, perhaps having become such after having suffered setbacks from the crypto world or having been the victim of a scam (who has not been raise his hand, I hold them low), who have however committed the error of accepting the definition given by Buterik without studying the reasons that push a user to recognize the practicality of a single secure protocol for the exchange of value between peers without reliable third parties.

This Bitcoin maximalism is not really such: I call it **BTC maximalism**, because the focus is the bitcoin asset rather than being the Bitcoin network.

From my point of view we should focus on Bitcoin and leave out the rest - the so-called crypto world - not (only) because the bitcoin asset is currently the only one with the possibility of being recognized as a global medium and Store of Value, but also, and above all, because the Bitcoin network is the only one that has the possibility of becoming a standard in the exchange of value between peers without a reliable third party.

If we analyze the history of the Internet, the only real term of comparison in the technological field, we see that actually several systems, each with its own rules, its protocols, competed with each other at the beginning. In this "cold war" between standards, who won according to you?

Not the permissioned and centralized corporate networks, but the open source and permissionless global network that we now know as the Internet.

But how did a system not imposed to prevail over perhaps even more efficient systems, mainly managed by a single entity, be it a company or a consortium or federation?

More than looking for the pure efficiency of the system in terms of speed and capacity, priority was given to the efficiency of communications and to what would become the purpose of the very existence of a global interconnection network: sharing.

Thus, on the one hand, there were intra-corporation networks, highly efficient, fast but closed, and on the other, slow research institutes' networks, but in communication with each other because they were open, willing to come together to define common communication standards.

Thus the latter prevailed and the suite of the Internet protocols that we still use today, called TCP/IP, was born, where IP indicates the Internet Protocol as the base layer (just above the physical network infrastructure), and TCP the Communication Protocol, that is the set of rules that define how the data packages shared by the network nodes must be managed.

The most open standard prevailed, which was not based on forced adoption but on shared intent.

Internet is just an example that shows how human beings tend to converge on well-defined standards; this convergence and sharing of intent is the basis of communication.

The same thing happens with the language: although there are multiple languages in the World, when we are dealing with a person who does not understand our mother tongue we tend to look for a new medium to be able to communicate, be it a lingua franca (typically a widely used language) or gestures.

And guess where we can see the same tendency to converge towards standards?

Exactly, in trades.

Gold is the medium par excellence, universally recognized as a scarce fine commodity, but even when we are dealing with fiat coins the subject does not change.

Let's take the Euro: many different countries, with different economic conditions, have decided to adhere to a single monetary standard in order to facilitate trade within the European Union. However, it is a pity that, although better than the previous models, this is not a good standard, precisely because it is imposed on the operators of the European economy, the single users, and not the result of a convergence of intents between individuals.

Can there be different protocols for exchanging value without a reliable third party competing with each other?

Of course they can exist, but, most likely, only one will remain and will constitute the so-called Settlement Layer for the exchanges of value on the Internet.

FOCUS 3

THE FUNDAMENTAL CHARACTERISTICS OF A BASIC TRUSTLESS PROTOCOL

A basic protocol for the exchange of value without a reliable third party must have characteristics similar to those that have defined the protocol for the global interconnection and that for the exchange of data packets, also without a reliable third party:

- (constant) decentralization
- (tendency to) immutability
- Safety
- Scalability/resilience
- Consensus

Right now the only system that can satisfy these features is Bitcoin.

My dear Ethereum supporters, unfortunately yours is not a useful system to build on it just because it violates all the features listed above.

Ripple? It lacks decentralization and therefore immutability and security, not to mention Consesus, but it is highly scalable.
Can it be a good basic protocol for the exchange of value without a third party? No, due to the lack of other necessary features.

Monero and Litecoin? They are approaching, but the trade-offs are such that, if the networks saturate, there would be a lack of decentralization due to the size that their blockchains would acquire (for Litecoin due to the size of the blocks, for Monero due to the architecture of the code, onchain-fungibility oriented).

FOCUS 4

COMPARISON BETWEEN TCP/IP AND LNP/BP

Before arriving at the definition of **LNP/BP** as a suite of protocols for the exchange of value among peers, let's see how the technology that instead allows us to exchange information (data) is composed and that is generically defined Internet.

The Internet is often displayed as a layered structure: it is customary to define this **TCP/IP** suite or stack.

The Internet Protocol suite was designed by Vinton G. Cerf and Robert E. Kahn while working on a communication systems development project funded by the Defense Advanced Research Project Agency (DARPA)[37].

The aim was to create a universal standard consisting of a series of communication protocols useful for the development of packet-switched networks. The TCP/IP suite was born, still used today.

Let's analyze it briefly.

APPLICATION LAYER

HTTP, IMAP, POP, NTP, SMB,
Whois, eDonkey, BitTorrent, etc.
... and Bitcoin

TRANSPORT LAYER
TCP, UDP, FCP, SCTP

INTERNET SETTLEMENT
(OR BASE) LAYER
Ip (Internet Protocol): eg. 192.168.1.1

PHYSICAL NETWORK ACCESS
Cable, Ethernet, Wifi, Satellite, ecc.

PHYSICAL NETWORK ACCESS represents the set of physical connections (transmission media) between the nodes of the network, on which the sequences of bits physically travel, converted into electrical signals.

The physical layer provides an electrical, mechanical and procedural interface to the transmission medium.[38]

INTERNET SETTLEMENT (OR BASE) LAYER establishes the logical connections between the nodes of the network. The Internet Protocol identifies the nodes via IP addresses (eg 192.168.1.1) and sends data packets from the source to the recipient. The Internet level can be defined as agnostic, as it routes the packets through different physical structures (ethernet, coaxial cable, wifi, etc.) and makes no distinction with respect to the levels above it, directing and routing data for different transport and application protocols.

TRANSPORT LAYER establishes the data channels used by the applications. The transport protocol can deal with error control, packet segmentation, flow control with packet sorting, congestion control and application addressing via the port number. The most widely used transport protocol is TCP, connection-oriented (Byte flow). Thanks to the TCP protocol:

- data arrives in order
- data has a minimal error
- duplicate data is deleted
- packets lost or discarded are sent back

includes traffic congestion control.[39]

TCP does not receive information about IP addresses. TCP's task is to get application-level data from one application to another reliably. The Internet Protocol has the task of obtaining data from one computer to another.[40]

APPLICATION LAYER groups all the applications that use the protocols contained in the TCP/IP suite in addition to the protocols used by the same applications, which define the operation and the possible connection with other applications.

Examples of application-level protocols include Hypertext Transfer Protocol (HTTP), File Transfer Protocol (FTP), Post Office Protocol (POP), Simple Mail Transfer Protocol (SMTP), but also BitTorrent (BT) and Bitcoin (BP).

We can now analyze how Bitcoin has evolved from an Application Layer software based on a P2P client/server sharing protocol to form itself a real Settlement Layer that presents characteristics of decentralization and "agnosticism" similar to those of the Internet Protocol.

We can have Bitcoin in a stack (or layer) structure similar to that of the TCP/IP suite, leaving out for the moment the PHYSICAL NETWORK ACCESS LAYER.

```
┌─────────────────────────────────────┐
│                                     │
│   APPLICATION LAYER                 │
│                                     │
│   RGB, Discreet Log Contracts, Storm│
│                                     │
│                                     │
├─────────────────────────────────────┤
│                                     │
│   TRANSPORT LAYER                   │
│   Lightning Network Protocol (LNP)  │
│                                     │
├─────────────────────────────────────┤
│                                     │
│   BITCOIN SETTLEMENT                │
│   (OR BASE) LAYER                   │
│   Bitcoin Protocol (BP):            │
│   e.g. address 36R4qFsySb73YnRWcAUj3vjfsR5Z34mgPj │
├─────────────────────────────────────┤
│                                     │
│   PHYSICAL NETWORK ACCESS           │
│   Cable, Ethernet, Wifi, Satellite, ecc. │
│                                     │
└─────────────────────────────────────┘
```

BITCOIN SETTLEMENT (OR BASE) LAYER establishes the logical connections between the nodes of the network as well as the basic rules of the network and monetary policy. The Bitcoin Protocol identifies the nodes through Internet public addresses (IP) or onion (Tor), and wallet through public addresses (eg 36R4qFsySb73YnRWcAUj3vjfsR5Z34mgPj) calculated by cryptographic hash functions starting from public keys, in turn calculated by means of an elliptic curve multiplication (ECDSA), and preserves the transactions occurring between source and recipient through a chain of transaction blocks that adopts the UTXO model.

The Bitcoin Layer can be defined as agnostic, as it routes transactions through different software implementations and makes no distinction with respect to the levels above it, directing and routing transactions for different transport and application protocols.

TRANSPORT LAYER stablishes the payment channels used by the applications. The Lightning Network transport protocol deals, among other things, with the creation of bidirectional peer payment channels, creation of Hashed Timelock Contracts, Decrementing Timelocks, Payment Routing and maintenance of Channel States.[41]

APPLICATION LAYER includes all the applications that use the protocols contained in the LNP/BP suite in addition to the protocols used by the same applications, which define the operation and the possible connection with other applications.

Examples of application-level protocols include RGB, Discreet Log Contracts[42] and Storm[43].

To sum up, **just as our data packets travel on second layers of the IP protocol, above all the TCP protocol, we can use second layers for the "transport" of our value**: LNP (Lightning Network Protocol) and others.

Viewing Bitcoin as a structured network in the form of a LNP/BP suite is useful for understanding the features of the various protocols and above all for developing solutions "on top of Bitcoin (Protocol)" without the need to constantly redefine the basic protocols or create new ones for exchanges of value without reliable third party.

It follows the uselessness of creating new blockchains in competition with Bitcoin Protocol unless we only want to redefine economic policy.

In this case, good luck and Consensus decides.

If we do not constantly redefine the basic protocols, since we already have decentralization and the (tendency to) immutability we need, and we focus on creating different applications and transaction layers, we can even realize the Austrian libertarian dream: to have private coins to be used in the free market, usable as cash, without a reliable third party. They are the so-called tokens, usable on top of the Base Layer, therefore not using the blockchain, as instead happens for example with Ethereum.

Not only coins: we can have simple coupons (utility tokens) but also security (with automatic management of dividends) without touching the Base Layer, relying exclusively on Application Layer solutions.

FOCUS 5

REDEFINING THE MONETARY UNIT

Recognized Bitcoin (or rather LNP/BP) as the only suite of reliable interconnection protocols between users wishing to exchange scarce digital value without resorting to centralized third parties, it is now necessary to solve a semantic problem.

How can we avoid the confusion created by the homonymy between the asset (bitcoin) and the system (Bitcoin)?

A first step could be to call bitcoin (asset) with its acronym (ticker) used in the market: **BTC**.

However, another element of confusion remains, always described above: *"these BTCs are too few and too expensive!"*
Furthermore, they are not at all suitable for micropayments, ie the vast majority of monetary transactions between individuals.

Therefore another unit of measure is needed, which fortunately already exists but has earned its name only after the disappearance of the Bitcoin project creator: **satoshi (sat)**.

Let's throw away all the various intermediate units, such as for example the bit (1 millionth of bitcoin, or 100 satoshis) and the mBTC (1 thousandth of bitcoin or 0.001 BTC) and use the basic units, which are understandable for the average user.

QUESTION 32

WHAT IS A REORG?

Bitcoin is a technology created to allow digital monetary transactions between two entities without relying on reliable third parties.

To do this it uses, among other things, a chain of blocks in order to keep track of transactions and to prevent someone from spending the same money twice.

We tend to think that the blockchain is an immutable ledger and this idea has spread to the point of assuming systems that make use of it without resorting to some kind of monetary transaction.

The idea has even spread that the concept of immutability applies to any blockchain, regardless of the number of nodes, the mining algorithm used (PoW, PoS, DPoS, etc.) and the "power" made available by miners and validators.

In fact, **no blockchain is immutable**, not even the Bitcoin's one.

Immutability is a characteristic that we tend to, never reach it at all: the way in which we try to approach it is what allows us to distinguish a functional, useful or useless blockchain.

Bitcoin is the most technically secure chain of blocks and therefore the one that most tends to be immutable.

Besides the (tendency to) immutability, another parameter to consider when looking for a functional timestamp block system (aka blockchain) is its neutrality, its agnosticism, as mentioned in the chapter *Comparison between TCP/IP and LNP/BP*.

So: **neutral technology, tending to immutability**.

Neutrality is achievable when the rules of the game are established before the start and do not change during the game, in fact they work to keep them tight, just like a referee does during a soccer match.

The referee, in the case of Bitcoin, is the code. But let us remember that this is written by human beings, who are fallible and make mistakes, so it may be necessary to put the code to hand in order to preserve the initial rules, making the code work as it should.

In some cases the "immutability" of the Bitcoin blockchain could be put at risk by a voluntary (or "coordinated") reorg.

A **reorg** is a common event for Bitcoin, to say the true, when it is not due to the will of an attacker: with "reorg" (or reorganization of the blockchain) we usually mean the event in which a client discovers a new correctly formed and longer blockchain than its reference chain and excludes one or more blocks that the client thought were part of the main blockchain. These excluded blocks become **orphans**.

In essence: I have a Bitcoin full node on my PC, my client realizes that the blockchain it is following is shorter than the one followed by the majority of nodes, so it stops following it and goes to the longer one. Consequently, if the one that followed has received transactions after the split, these will be considered invalid.

If you remember we talked about a similar event in the chapter *What happens to the miners who lose the race?*.

In that chapter it was said that the miners receive the block containing the solution provided by the miner who is supposed to be the winner and verify it, like all the other full nodes.
If the block is valid, they immediately stop working on the solution to the

previous problem and start working on a new problem, contained within this new block.

If, however, they do not notice in time the presence of a valid solution, they will continue their work on the current block.
In this case, it may happen that a miner discovers the solution after the first miner; he will send its candidate block to the network and it will be rejected. His client will realize that he has mined on a shorter chain, because the main one has meanwhile gone ahead and the miners have started working on it. He will therefore accept the defeat and will understand that the bitcoins that he has awarded as a prize are not valid, as are the fees contained in the transactions inside his block; the block he discovered will become an "orphan" and he will start working on the longest blockchain.

However, it may happen that someone tries a voluntary reorg of the chain, in order to invalidate transactions and assign bitcoins that are not due to him.

Take this situation in which every reference is purely coincidental: an exchange we will call "Finance" suffers the theft of a few thousand bitcoins, due to its inefficient security measures.
These stolen bitcoins are used by the hacker for many different reasons: buying a Lambo, paying for coffee, keeping them for the future.
In short, they are part of the system and are used in some transactions.

The owner of Finance, this BhangQeng Vhao (BV), gets a suggestion from a programmer who has worked on Bitcoin:
"*if you reveal your private keys for the hacked coins (or a subset of them) you can decentralized-ly at zero cost to you, coordinate a reorg to undo the theft.*"
BV thinks it is a good idea to modify the entire network ledger to cancel the theft and repair an error made by its exchange.

Big deal.

Technically it is possible: he needs to convince the majority of the mining pools, and therefore of the miners connected to them, to work on an alternative blockchain to the main one. The miners should begin to mine the shorter blockchain, the one in which the bitcoins were not stolen from Finance and moved by the hacker.

In short, they should rewrite history.

Of course, to do so they should have some economic incentive. Some miner should in fact renounce the reward obtained thanks to the blocks following the theft, plus all the transaction fees.

Let us imagine that the theft occurred at 8.00 am and that BV proposes the reorg at 12.00.
Four hours have passed, approximately 23 blocks from what we consider as block 0, the block containing the "theft" transaction.
Miners, after the block 0, obtained 287.5 bitcoins, without considering transaction fees.
If the single bitcoin is worth 10,000 USD, it means $ 2,875,000 in rewards. For a reorg that cancels the thief's transaction, the block that contains it must also be reorganized, so the miners have to work on 24 blocks, giving up 300 bitcoins, excluding fees, or a value in USD of 3 million.

BV must hurry to convince the miners: every 10 minutes a block is added to the chain, so the costs increase rapidly!
It is logical to think that the owner of Finance could take a few days to organize a global reorg event: even if he has the possibility to contact the mining pools directly, it is a matter of making sure that the miners who support it are actually favorable to this initiative. Everyone would see their compensation canceled, and would remain with the sole hope that after the reorg the mining pool will distribute the new rewards.
If a few days pass, as is actually probable, BV should convince the miners with an incentive of a few thousand bitcoins, perhaps even higher than what was stolen from its exchange!

Let's imagine that he succeeds and that he convinces the vast majority of the pools to mine a version of the chain without the "theft" transaction.

The single bitcoin, the asset of a monetary system that is no longer resistant to censorship, would lose value drastically: the systemic (economic) crash would lead the miners to remain with a handful of useless digital collector's items.

Therefore they would have given up bitcoins obtained with extreme effort, useful to repay the expenses they sustained in terms of electricity for work and for the dissipation of the generated heat, wear and tear of the machinery, employees, etc. and to make a profit, and in return have obtained bitcoins which are always valid but which by now are unlikely to have an economic value because the system has lost one of the basic characteristics to which it has always tended, the non-reversibility of transactions.

So any reorg is bad for Bitcoin?

We have said that technology is designed to be neutral and prone to immutability. We have also stated that the referee is the code and not the will of the individuals who intend to change the system for personal interests.

This code, however, being written by humans, may be somewhat flawed.

Imagine that an attacker finds an error in the code that allows him to create a few million bitcoins out of the thin air.
The rules of the game state that it is not possible to create more bitcoins than expected for each block, that this amount is halved every four years from the start of the "game" and that there is a limit to the creation of new coins (the famous 21 million bitcoins).

If a flaw allowed us to violate these initial rules then we would have a problem. The developer community will have to get to work and ensure that the code respects the rules for which it was designed.

Let's say the attacker actually applied his discovery and generated 40 million bitcoins, but they could also be 1 satoshi more than the expected reward. These bitcoins could be used to make transactions.
Is it right therefore to push for a reorg of the blockchain that cancels these

transactions, after that a new code without bugs has been issued?
From my point of view, a voluntary reorg is always wrong but there are those who say that, in this case, it would be a "restore to factory conditions", that is to a code that does what it was created for.
This would ultimately be an error to be corrected, not a subjective change, the result of a political choice.

Take the example of a card game: one of the players hides jokers up his sleeve and decides to play them when it suits him.
The cards are more than the initial ones and the rules are violated by a striker, even if ultimately the mistake is of the dealer who did not prevent the cheater from starting.

In the initial example, instead, it is an initiative that does not have to do with preserving the rules of the network but with personal interests that place the community in front of a political choice.

During the Bitcoin story several bugs have been discovered, three of which were very critical.
In 2010 a bug was discovered in block 74638 which led to the creation of 184,467,440,737.09551616 bitcoins to three addresses.
Five hours after the discovery, Satoshi Nakamoto released a patch (a soft fork) that was going to insert a modification to the network rules: any transaction with more than 21 million bitcoins would henceforth be rejected by the network.
At the time the single bitcoin had recently gained an economic value and there were no consequences for users.
In 2013 the blockchain split again due to another bug. The situation was restored to normal around 6 hours later and there was a single double spending attack against OKPay. In 2018, yet another critical bug was discovered by a Bitcoin Cash developer and communicated to the main Bitcoin Core developers, who released a patch after 5 hours.

The Consensus decided in 2010 to continue the chain whose economic rules were those originally established, effectively canceling transactions that did not respect the limit of 21 million bitcoins, and in 2013 to roll back to a previous version of the protocol. If those reorgs had not been realized, it is not possible to know what the consequences would have been in terms of future reliability of the system and economic value of the asset and if an attempt to reorg of this type happened now, we do not know what the consequences could be in terms of Consensus and value of the bitcoin asset.

Luckly, the two events took place at an early stage in the history of Bitcoin, in which the asset did not yet have an important economic value and in which the number of nodes was extremely small.

QUESTION 33

What are the main critical points of Bitcoin?

Bitcoin is an innovative and decentralized system, not only in the management of nodes but also in terms of development.

Its being open source makes it possible for anyone to work on it and to propose subsequent modifications to the protocol to the community.

Some detractors of the system, who usually support alternative and definetly less decentralized and neutral systems, argue that a sort of programmer lobby has "appropriated" the project and pushed it in the direction they set.

This point of view is born from a misunderstanding: **Bitcoin is a decentralized network but there are limited software implementations that allow its use in accordance with the basic protocol.**

The main of these implementations is Bitcoin Core, created by the same Nakamoto.
Since the disappearance of Nakamoto, but to tell the truth, even before that, the management of the development of Bitcoin Core has been entrusted to some programmers and a lead maintainer, to date Wladimir J. van der Laan. For a complete overview of how Bitcoin Core development works, please take a look at the article *Who Controls Bitcoin Core?* by Jameson Lopp. [22]

Core is not Bitcoin though.

As mentioned, anyone, in compliance with the basic protocol, can develop their own full node software.

The "Bitcoin Core" name, used to define the system, it is a clear attempt to confuse users by trying to convince them of an alleged centralization of the system.

Remember that, even assuming that a centralization in the development of Bitcoin exists, it is the nodes that have the final "right to vote". At each update, anyone with a node can decide whether they agree with the new implementation and whether to support the changes by installing it.

Bitcoin is a system that is still relatively young and in full development but, with the passage of time and blocks, it becomes more and more solid.

Far from being perfect!

There are still critical issues; some concern the onchain scalability of the system, which will be improved over time, others its exposure to possible attacks, some the block mining protocol and others the decentralization of its development.

In this book we have verified that the economic model underlying Bitcoin discourages attacks on the network (eg a voluntary reorg with the complicity of more than half of the miners) which, even if possible, would constitute a losing bet: a Bitcoin system sensitive to these attacks would see its currency drastically losing value and the attacking miners would risk remaining with a handful of useless digital collectible objects in their hands.

We can therefore deduce that the more the system is strengthened in terms of the computing power employed by the miners (hashrate), the number of miners and the monetary value of the bitcoin asset, the less it is likely that coordinated attacks against it will take effect.

Regarding onchain scalability, that is the possibility of increasing the number of transactions that can be performed on blockchain, different solutions are being studied.

Although second layer solutions such as Lightning Network are considered by most to be the correct way to exponentially increase the number of transactions, it is also true that these will necessarily have to be accompanied by blockchain scaling solutions.

The introduction of SegWit paved the way for Lightning Network and, as a pleasant side effect, "lightened" onchain transactions, but not enough. Therefore, important modifications to the basic protocol are being developed that will constitute, in the coming years, the backbone on which future scaling solutions will be implemented:

1. **Schnorr signatures**, proposed by the co-founder of Blockstream Pieter Wuille, which would allow various participants to produce a single aggregated signature with a single public key;
2. **Merkelized Abstract Syntax Trees (MAST)**, proposed by the Bitcoin Core developer Dr.Johnson Lau, which would reduce the size of smart contract on blockchain;
3. **Taproot**, which would combine these two above to improve the privacy of single Bitcoin transactions.

> "Taproot to make all outputs and cooperative spends indistinguishable from each other. Merkle branches to hide the unexecuted branches in scripts. Schnorr signatures enable wallet software to use key aggregation/thresholds within one input."
> - Pieter Wuille

A further technological step will be given by the much reviled increase in the size of the Bitcoin blocks.

Let us remember that the limit to the weight of the single block is an imposed but common sense measure, designed to preserve the decentralization of the system itself.

As we have seen previously, an increase in size without appropriate and obvious technological improvements, including the expansion of hard disk storage capacity and the increase in capacity and available bandwidth (throughput) of user connections, would entail a rapid centralization of system because fewer individuals would be able to maintain active full nodes. The number of nodes would initially be concentrated in the most technologically advanced areas of the world, reducing to those with higher technological barriers. It would then end up with a dangerous "professionalization" of Bitcoin block validation and the system would lose its main purpose.

Therefore it will be possible to proceed with an increase in the size of the blocks when any threat to decentralization is avoided.

Let us now analyze the critical issues concerning Bitcoin mining.

Today most of the miners cooperate with each other within pools: the more the difficulty increases and the more it does it in a short time, the greater this tendency to cooperation. As we saw in the mining chapter, the individual miner should be mine along with others because his chances of discovering the solution that allows him to close the block are extremely rare: it is better to solve many small problems at a time and communicate the result to the pool, rather than trying to solve everything alone.

The problem lies in the fact that, in theory, those who have control of the pools could hijack the computing power of the system for personal purposes: support this or that version of the protocol (forks), collaborate with other great actors to rewrite the history of the transactions (voluntary reorgs), and so on.

Stratum V1, the mining protocol used by the vast majority of pools, therefore offers them a relatively powerful position.
Not only are they responsible for distributing rewards to miners, but they have decision-making power over which transactions to include in the candidate blocks, as well as on which version of the Bitcoin Protocol to use.[44]

Solutions are therefore being studied that would drastically reduce the impact this cooperative management has on the decentralization of Bitcoin mining.

Betterhash

Betterhash, a solution developed by Matt Corallo, was designed to reduce the dominant position of pool operators: if implemented it would allow individual miners to build their candidate blocks by themselves, independently deciding which transactions to include, as well as maintaining personal full node, with the consequent possibility to choose which version of the Bitcoin Protocol to support.

Betterhash would therefore provide more efficiency, security and decentralization to mining pools.[45]

According to some, the solution proposed by Matt Corallo would not completely eliminate the potential abuse of dominant positions by the pool administrators: these could still force the miners to censor some transactions with the threat of not receiving rewards if they did not.

That being said, a threatened miner could simply change pools.

Stratum V2

Braiins, the company behind Slush Pool, recently announced the second version of Stratum, Stratum V2.
This is a solution inspired by Betterhash, which solves many of the problems of the first version as well as some critical aspects of Matt Corallo's proposal.

In an interview with Bitcoin Magazine, Braiins co-CEO Pavel Moravec explained that:

"Stratum V2 would allow pool operators to verify the validity of new block models asynchronously. As soon as a miner sends a candidate block to the pool, he can immediately start hashing. Meanwhile, the pool operator starts checking all the new candidate blocks.

If a block model is later deemed invalid, the miners' reward can be modified accordingly. So the miners have an incentive to work on adequate blocks and provide all the data in a timely manner. However, they can continue to work on their candidate blocks without any delay."

Stratum V2 would also introduce other improvements in security, efficiency and flexibility. After numerous internal tests on Slush Pool, Braiins will submit its solution to the community by publishing a Bitcoin Improvement Proposal (BIP).

Let's finish by spending a few words on the decentralization of Bitcoin development.

While considering that, as mentioned, the development of Bitcoin is in the hands of the free initiative of programmers around the world, it is also true that, if we observe which implementations of full node software are more used, Bitcoin Core turns out to be the most widespread, present on about 97% of the nodes.[46]

Lightning Network's implementations, which allow us to configure LN nodes and actively interact with the network, are more decentralized in their development and use than those of the Bitcoin base layer.

In just over a year since the development of the Lightning Network mainet we have eight implementations available:

1. LND (go)

2. c-lightning (c)

3. Eclair (scala)

4. Electrum (python)

5. Ptarmigan (c)

6. BLW (scala)

7. Rust-Lightning (rust)

8. Lpd (rust)

I therefore consider it appropriate that work on alternative versions of Bitcoin Core should continue unabated, for the sake of the Bitcoin base layer itself: more versions available reduce the likelihood of critical bugs occurring and that DDoS-type attacks on Bitcoin Core may endanger network decentralization.

Appendix I - Best Practices

Don't trust, verify!
Always check that the software you use to manage your bitcoins does what it says it does. Prefer open source solutions instead of proprietary software, precisely because these can be tested by independent developers.

Never share your private keys, for any reason and with any person. Not your keys, not your bitcoins.

Don't keep your wealth on a custodial wallet or any other third-party service. You do not own private keys and the system is subjected to the issues of classic centralized systems. Transfer the your funds to an offline wallet (cold wallet) carefully stored and protected from external attacks.

Stay away from the Get-rich-quick schemes, in which someone promises you strong earnings and in a short time: these include the famous Ponzi schemes (or pyramid schemes), in which enriching ones is who is at the top of the pyramid and exploits the investments of who is below, promising them substantial profits but actually redistributing only part of the money coming from the new affiliates.

Never invest more than you are willing to lose. It is valid for any area, not only for a new technology like Bitcoin.

Remember that Lightning Network is a still experimental technology that could still have many critical bugs. If you want to test its features make sure you use a few satoshis.

Consolidate the outputs of an onchain transaction
With the increase in the value of the single bitcoin and the reduction of premiums for miners due to halving, it will be increasingly difficult to

execute blockchain transactions that move few satoshis: the price of the fee may be greater than the total amount transacted.

The bitcoins on an address that cannot be moved because the commissions are greater than the same, are called dust: they can be the result of change or satoshis "collected" in microtransactions.
Imagine that a user has several bitcoin addresses - which is common if you use a deterministic hierarchical wallet - and that many of them are dust.
The user could have a significant amount of satoshis if he sums up all these funds but is not able to use them!

So here is the need to consolidate transaction outputs.

In times when the mempoils are almost empty it is good practice to collect all these dust and send them, in a single transaction, to an address belonging to us. Dust (the outputs) will therefore constitute the inputs of a single transaction that constitutes the actual balance sheet of the user.

In Bitcoin Core the procedure is quite simple:
prepare a new outgoing transaction and select the reception wallet (one of your own, even inside Bitcoin Core). Then click on Coin Control - if you don't see the button you have to activate this function through the general settings - and select all the various outputs.
Now in the Amount field you enter the maximum available, net of the fees you wish to pay.
The various outputs will consolidate and, when funds arrive at your receiving address, you will see a single one in Coin Control.
If you want to consolidate the funds on your light wallet, the procedure is just as simple: just send yourself the maximum amount (max amount), always remembering to establish the fees you wish to pay first.
This technique is therefore useful in view of a future increase in Bitcoin fees, but consider that it could lead to a privacy problem, especially if you use an address previously used in the past or if the funds do not pass through a mixing system.

If on the one hand consolidating the outputs allows for lighter transactions and therefore less expensive in terms of commissions, on the other it exposes to privacy problems.

Let's imagine consolidating all our 0.01 bitcoin wallet outputs and having to spend, as before, 0.001 BTC for the purchase of a good or service: the seller will not see only 0.0015 BTC as in the example above. , but he will be able to know the entire balance of our wallet, because to make the payment we will have to send all our money (a single UTXO) of 0.01 BTC and receive the rest.

If we made a parallelism with bank transfers, it is as if the shopkeeper who has to receive a transfer, sees our entire balance instead of just the requested amount.

Therefore, remember this compromise when you want to consolidate your outputs and, possibly, divide your wallets: what you use for expenses (hot wallet) should always be different from what contains your savings (cold wallet).

Appendix II - Business modeling in the Bitcoin Lightning Network Ecosystem, by Federico Spitaleri (satoshis.games)

Introduction

This article aims at providing Lapps (Lightning Network applications) with valuable insights about the Lightning Network ecosystem that will help them to build a successful business model.

We'll go through the major sections of a Business Model Canvas and present some case studies of Lapps that already operate in the market. We'll have a look at what resources are necessary for Lapps to operate, what is their value proposition, how they deliver their value proposition to their target market and finally how they monetize.

It is important to mention that Lightning users still represent a very small market niche, therefore many of the models presented here would require more Lightning Network users in order to become profitable. However, designing a business model that not only uses a trending technology but also does that in a scalable way is a good practice in order to prepare for when the niche of Lightning users will be big enough to allow Lapps to generate significant profits.

Business models in the Lightning ecosystem

A business model describes how organizations create, deliver and gather value. It also identifies key interactions and collaborations with suppliers, customers and other actors that operate in the market.

In the present paragraph we're going to explore the new value propositions that the Lightning Network brings, the ways those value propositions are delivered to the customers, the resources that are necessary for Lapps to operate in the market, the costs that Lapps have to bear and finally the available options for Lapps to make revenue.

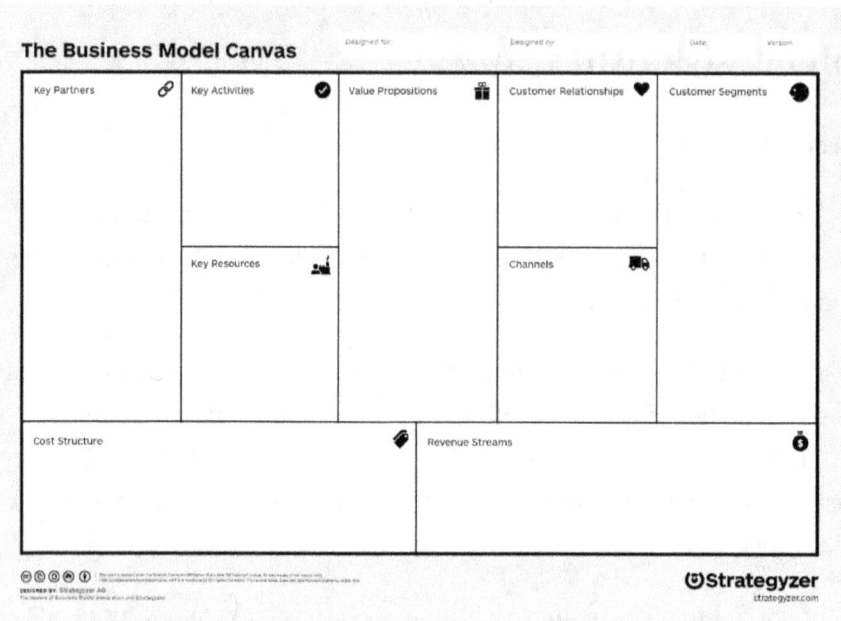

Business Model Canvas. Source: strategyzer.com

Value proposition

It represents the value that Lapps offer to their target market. When startups build a Lapp they need to ask them-selves the following questions: what was impossible before the advent of the Lightning Network?
How can their Lapp make it possible?
What can their Lapp do more efficiently/effectively than other companies that offer the same product/service but don't use the Lightning Network?
Does their Lapp solve any problem/satisfy any need?

Let's start by making a list of features that the Lightning Network offers; we'll then have a look at some examples of Lapps' value propositions.

Lightning Network's features:

4. Instant and cheap transferring of value;
5. Micro-transactions;
6. Private transactions;
7. Automatic withdrawal of **any amount** (even fractions of Euro cents) **at any time**;
8. New methods for authenticating users (proof-of-payment and digital signatures based on Node IDs)

Examples of Lapps' value propositions:

Tippin.me: it allows people to send and receive tips in an easy, cheap and instant way. In addition, tips can be very small (fractions of Euro cents) so that the sender can tip any amount and the receiver can accumulate those amounts and withdraw at any time. Through a browser extension it is also possible to tip tweets on Twitter by clicking on a specific icon next to the "like" button;

Satoshis.games: it allows users to earn Bitcoin by playing games. Within the gaming platform, the transferring of value is not unidirectional (from the user to the platform: pay-to-play system) but bidirectional (from the user to the platform and from the platform to the user). Satoshis.games uses Bitcoin as a currency within the games, so that such currency is not platform-dependent and the in-game micro-economy is not fictitious (value can be extracted from the platform and spent on other Lapps or in everyday life). Finally, digital elements within the games (e.g. Super Mario coins) have a real value and such value can be instantly withdrawn at any time and at zero cost. Every digital action on Satoshis.games can be monetized or rewarded;

Gab: it's a fork of the Brave browser. Gab's team is working on an implementation that will pay users for watching advertisements while browsing the web. The advantage on the users' side is that they can be rewarded even for a "micro-usage" of the browser and such remuneration is paid through a "real time" micro-transaction that can be withdrawn at any time;

<u>Sats 4 Likes</u>: it's a Lapp that rewards users for sharing and liking posts on social media. Companies or individuals that want to advertise their products on social media publish a task on Sats 4 Likes and specify how much users will be paid for sharing/liking/commenting a post. They then pay an invoice to Sats 4 Likes which then pays the users when they complete the task. The value proposition consists in rewarding "micro-tasks" with micro-transactions (fair enough), making advertisers pay for concrete, valuable and specific actions instead of impressions or clicks. In addition, Sats 4 Likes represents a channel through which it's possible to target Bitcoin and Lightning Network users in a very direct and effective manner: rewarding users only with Bitcoin allows solely for Bitcoin users to be reached. Targeting Bitcoiners on traditional channels is instead very complicated as social media like Facebook, Instagram and Twitter cannot provide such detailed targeting parameters able to optimize the budget reaching only actual Bitcoin users;

<u>Suredbits</u>: it provides access to historical and real-time streaming data feeds. Thanks to the Lightning Network, their services are priced at a micro level: customers pay only for the data they want to use (no monthly or annual contracts) and nothing more.

Lightning Network ecosystem. Source: J. Dantoni 2019, The Block Genesis

Channels

Through the channels, Lapps must deliver their value proposition. Channels represent the link to the customers, the way Lapps reach them. Depending on the product, channels can be web applications accessible directly from the web or any app store in case Lapps are mobile or desktop applications.

A channel that is very specific for the Lightning Network ecosystem is the Bluewallet marketplace. Lapps that want to be reached directly from where Bitcoiners spend their money (the Bluewallet app) can ask to be listed on the marketplace of the wallet mentioned above.

Other channels that are specific for the industry at hand are represented by web based marketplaces such as lightningnetworkstores.com and Lightning Hood. There is also a newsletter service, lapps.co, which delivers updates about new Lapps on the market: startups can contact them and be included in the updates.

A very effective channel through which it's possible to execute advertising campaigns for promoting Lapps is Sats 4 Likes. As we previously mentioned, this marketing channel makes it very easy to only reach Lightning Network users and helps to avoid spending marketing budgets on clicks and impressions from users that don't use Lightning and may be included in the target audience on Twitter, Facebook and Google campaigns.

Customer relationships

Customer relationship channels are the channels through which Lapps should maintain the relationship with their customers/users, offer customer support and send follow-up messages, notifications and everything else that is necessary in order to retain the customers and satisfy their needs.
The most used customer relationship channels in the Lightning Network ecosystem are Telegram and Slack for customer support and Twitter for promotion and customer engagement.

Customer segments

Based on data from the network (number of active nodes) and app stores (number of downloads of the main wallets that support LN) we can estimate a population of a few tens of thousands of LN users. Any Lapp's target market is a subset of that population (e.g. gamers among LN users, if a Lapp operates in the gaming industry; music streamers among LN users, if a Lapp operates in the music streaming industry).

As we already said during the introduction, there are still very few LN users but testing the business model within the current market niche makes Lapps ready for when adoption will spread and making significant profits will be feasible.

Revenue streams

How do Lapps make revenue? This really depends on the product. However, there are some models that can be taken as examples:

- in-app purchases: they represent one of Satoshis.games' revenue streams. This model consists in allowing users to purchase in-app contents such as lives, games features, avatars, etc;
- fees: Lapps can charge fees when purchases are made. This is the case of Sats 4 Likes, where companies or individuals decide to invest a certain amount of Bitcoin in advertising a post on social media and Sats 4 Likes charges them extra satoshis for the service;
- pay per use: this is a model that really fits with the Lightning Network technology. Infact, micro-transactions allow businesses to price their services at a micro-level so that they can charge their customers even for a "micro-usage" of the service and only for what they consume. This model replaces subscription plan models where users are charged a fixed fee, regardless if they used the service for an entire month or just for few hours. This is the model used by Suredbits, the data streaming service;

- freemium: it consists in giving users free access to an application with minimum features. Users who want premium features will have to pay for them or purchase a premium account. This is also the case of Satoshis.games, where users can play Super Bro for free and buy additional lives and features if they want to have more chances to win;
- Advertising: Lapps that want to make revenues through advertising need to take some issues into account. Bitcoin users care much about their privacy, they don't like being spied on: advertising on Lapps should not be very intrusive and data about users should have a certain degree of anonymity. This will lead to less detailed targeting for advertisers and probably to a lower price of the advertising space. However, doing so Lapps will preserve their community and keep their customer base loyal.

Cost structure

Lapps' cost structure does not really change in comparison to traditional business models. It includes development costs (salaries for developers), IT maintenance costs (costs of the server of the website), marketing costs, bureaucratic costs (tax advisors, lawyers, consultants and other services) and so on. If a Lapp's Lightning Network node has been launched through BTCPay server and uses a cloud hosting service like LunaNode, the Lapp will also have to take into account the cost of that service (around 10€/month).

Key resources

Key resources refer to those resources that make a Lapp difficult to imitate or replicate. They really depend on the product. Here instead, I'm going to list the two main resources that every Lapp needs to operate in the Lightning Network ecosystem:

- a Lightning Network node, running for example on BTCPay server or on a RaspiBlitz;

- inbound capacity (for receiving payments). It can be obtained through a Lightning Network channel-opening service like Thor;

If a Lapp wants to avoid launching its own node, it can integrate Lightning through services like APItoshi by Satoshis Games and OpenNode.

We'll skip the Key Activities section as they depend entirely on the type of product/service.

Key partners

The Lightning Network ecosystem is a very collaborative space. Startups should take advantage of that and partner up with other businesses in order to leverage synergies, increase brand awareness and accessibility to their Lapp.

A potential key partner of every Lightning Network application is surely represented by Bluewallet. Bluewallet is one of the most popular Bitcoin wallets that support the Lightning Network and from its marketplace it is possible to access many Lapps. Startups can partner up with Bluewallet and list their Lapp on its marketplace. This way Lapps will be one step closer to their customers (Lightning users) and Bluewallet will benefit from that by offering more purchase occasions to its customers. Same thing with those marketplaces that we mentioned in the "Channels" paragraph (lightningnetworkstores.com, Lightning Hood, etc): startups can list their Lapp there to gain brand awareness and traffic, and those marketplaces will be able to offer more contents to their users.

Validating the business model

Drawing a business model on a piece of paper is not enough: business models need to be validated through intensive testing.
Here we introduce the Lean methodology, which consists of 3 main steps:

1. Creating a MVP based on market insights: a MVP (minimum viable product) is the simplest version of a product that tries to satisfy the customer needs. For example: if a company's goal is to create a product that allows people to move from point A to point B without walking, its MVP will not be a car nor a bike but a skateboard. Only essential features should be built to stay Agile during the validation process. It is very important to build those features based on market insights: development must be driven by customer research;
2. MVP testing and performance measurement: the MVP must be launched on the market to see if it gets traction. Metrics like sales, traffic volume and customer retention need to be measured;
3. Going forward or pivoting: if metrics show a good performance, the product can be improved by adding more features and running more tests (the circle starts again, with improvements on the previous MVP). If metrics show a bad performance, it probably means that the value proposition is not perceived as valuable by the customers or that the business model is not able to generate and gather value so it needs to be redesigned. At this point it is necessary to pivot: the startup needs to listen to the customer needs again, build a new value proposition and a new MVP that must be tested. The development of the new MVP should start after deeply researching about the customer needs.

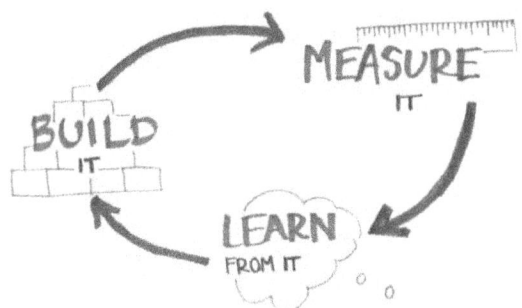

Lean Methodology

Conclusions

If Lapps want to be successful in the long term, they need a proper business model that allows them to deliver their value proposition to their customers and be profitable.

In this article we provided some insights about the Lightning Network ecosystem that could help Lapps to build a successful business model.

In the long term, only those Lapps that will satisfy actual needs in a sustainable way will turn out to be successful when LN adoption will spread.

Contacts

Need help in designing your business model or in advertising your Lapp through the right channels?

Send a message to:
email: federico@satoshis.games
Twitter: @FedericoSpital3

Appendix III – One CPU, one vote. A widespread misconception

"One CPU, one vote" is a widespread misunderstanding, due to a misinterpretation of the following statement by Satoshi Nakamoto, contained in the Bitcoin withepaper: *"If the majority were based on one-IP-address-one-vote, it could be subverted by anyone able to allocate many IPs. Proof-of-work is essentially one-CPU-one-vote. The majority decision is represented by the longest chain, which has the greatest proof-of-work effort invested in it. If a majority of CPU power is controlled by honest nodes, the honest chain will grow the fastest and outpace any competing chains."*

First of all, the above statement is often extrapolated and used out of context. Nakamoto was, in this case, describing how Proof of Work works (section 4 of the whitepaper), not the Bitcoin Protocol.

Let's take for good the fact that in Bitcoin there is a "democratic vote", which is actually not true, as we have seen in the chapter *What is a Bitcoin fork?*.

When Nakamoto elaborated the phrase "One CPU, one vote", the conditions were as follows:

1) the only relevant case of Proof of Work applied to an electronic cash system was that of Hal Finney's RPoW, applied to his digital money project. Prior to this, PoW was simply used as an anti-spam system.

2) PoW used the CPU for brute force calculations: the more powerful the CPU the more calculations you could make. The more CPU you had available, the greater your weight (the so-called "vote") in the Proof of Work system.

3) No one had yet used GPUs nor invented the ASICs, so Nakamoto linked the increase in the mining difficulty ONLY to the increase in the number of CPUs and to the performance of the latter (Moore's law).

4) Full node were validators but also miners. If you didn't want to mine with your hardware, you had to disable this feature.

To date, the miners are not validators (due to Stratum V1), but will again be able to do so in the future thanks to Stratum V2 (see chapter *What are the main critical points of Bitcoin?*). In any case they would not have a greater role in the Consensus but would extend the mining decentralization.

5) Miners do not have a prevalent role on the Consensus but are at the service of the validator nodes. For this service they receive a monetary incentive consisting of subsidy + fees (reward). In the case of a hard fork they adapt to the chain that has Consensus because they are driven by profit, not by goodness or democracy.

To understand why they have no decision-making power, see the case of Segwit2x (from a proposal supported by large mining pools) and the lack of adoption of this proposal by the community.

As we have said, however, with the phrase "one CPU, one vote", Satoshi Nakamoto was referring to a single component of Bitcoin, the Proof of Work, and not to the entire operation of the system; therefore the conditions expressed above are completely superfluous in that context and only serve to understand that applying this sentence to the entire Bitcoin Protocol is incorrect.

Appendix IV – How much does it cost to send bitcoins?

One of the myths about Bitcoin to dispel is related to the cost per transaction (mining fees).
Specifically, the myth is: " The higher the transaction amount, the higher the commission spend. "
This misunderstanding is probably due to what happens with classic payment systems, especially with cross-border payments: a commission is usually paid as a percentage of the transaction.

With Bitcoin, things work differently: you could potentially find yourself in the situation where transferring a billion dollars in bitcoin costs less than transferring a few USD."

Why?

When we transfer bitcoins, our wallet constructs the transaction, aggregating the quantities of available BTC.

Let's imagine our Bitcoin wallet as a classic cash wallet. Inside we have some 10 euro banknotes, some 20, some coins and so on, for a total of 130 euros.

If we had to pay for a good or service that costs 100 euros, we should obviously add up the various banknotes until we reach the required amount. If we exceed the amount and pay, we will get a change (if for example we pay with a 50 euro banknote and three 20 euro banknotes).

In Bitcoin the procedure is very similar: those previously defined "amount of available bitcoins" are actually called unspent outputs (UTXO) and become, all or part of the inputs of our transaction, that is the "banknotes" that will go to form the total transaction.

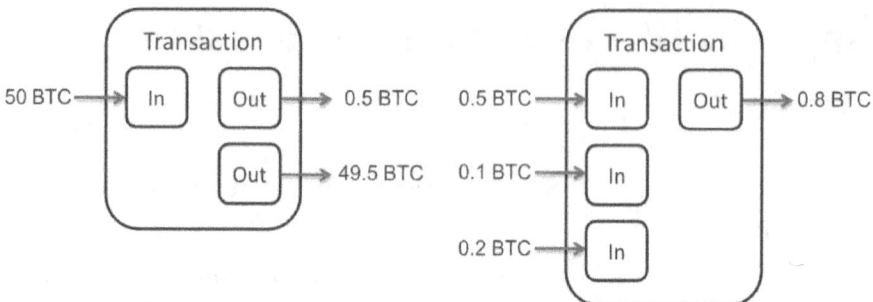

On the left, a transaction that uses a single UTXO as input, on the right a transaction that uses multiple UTXOs as input and transfers the total to a single output. Source: https://commons.wikimedia.org/wiki/File:Bitcoin_Transaction_Inputs_and_Outputs.png

Let's imagine we have a total of 0.01 bitcoins in our wallet - or 1'000'000 satoshis, if we prefer to think with this unit of measurement -, equal to around 80 euros the moment I'm writing. However, these bitcoins are the result of many unspent outputs, because we received about ten transactions of different amounts for them.

In the event that we have to pay for a good / service costing 100,000 satoshis (0.001 BTC), our wallet will take our "cash" and add them up to obtain a sum equal to or greater than the amount due.

Let's assume that the total sum is 0.0015 BTC and is the result of 4 UTXO added together: we will pay 0.0015 BTC, 0.001 BTC will go to the seller while 0.0005 BTC will return to our wallet, and will constitute a single unspent output.

Then, recap:

1. we had 0.01 BTC (balance sheet) consisting of a dozen UTXOs: 0.0002 BTC + 0.0007 BTC + 0.0001 BTC + 0.0005 BTC + ...
2. The wallet sums the first four UTXOs and gets 0.0015 BTC.

3. It pays this 0.0015 BTC to a seller, get back a single UTXO of 0.0005 BTC (change), which adds up to the other outputs that make up the total remaining balance.

A transaction consisting of many inputs has a weight in bytes greater than one with few or even a single input. **We do not pay based on the amount of bitcoins moved, rather it can be said that we pay based on the amount of unspent output that we are going to use as an input to our transaction.**

Commissions to miners are paid in sats per byte (or sats/vbyte for SegWit commissions).

Let's assume we want to pay 4 sats / byte because we are in a situation where there is no congestion in the Bitcoin network and we are pretty sure that our transaction will be confirmed within a few hours, becoming part of the transactional history of the transaction chain (blockchain).

A good wallet allows, among other things, to manually set the commissions , so let's select 4 sats / byte and choose the amount to pay.

In Edge Wallet we can determine which commissions to use, choosing from High, Standard, Low or Custom. With this last option we can specify the fees in sats/byte.

Since we have a lot of inputs, our transaction will have an important weight and those 4 sats/bytes could lead to a relatively high total cost in commissions.

For example, if our transaction had a weight of 400 bytes, we would end up paying 1,600 satoshis (4 x 400 bytes).

Our 0.0001 BTC transaction will therefore have a commission of 1,600 satoshis (0.00001600 BTC).

Now let's imagine that we are a millionaire and want to transact 1,000,000 euros in BTC, or about 124.5 bitcoins today. If we had these bitcoins in a single unspent output, our transaction will have the least possible weight: let's assume 200 bytes.

With the same sats/bytes, therefore, this transaction will involve a commission cost of only 800 satoshis (4 x 200 bytes), compared to 1,600 satoshis of the previous one.

So with 800 satoshis (0.064 euros), we moved 1 million euros in bitcoin, while previously with 1,600 satoshis (0.13 euros) we only moved 80 euros.

In the first we spent 0.1625% on commissions, in the 1 million euros transaction we spent the 0.0000064%.

We therefore understand that moving 1, 100 or 1 million bitcoins makes no difference, as long as you have a transaction with the same weight in bytes.

How can we spend as little as possible on commissions?

First of all, as mentioned previously, we must choose a wallet that gives us the possibility to set a custom commission; therefore we discard all those who do not give us this possibility.

Another useful tip is to have a small number of unspent outputs within the wallet, but the latter does not always allow us to know which and how many UTXOs make up our total balance.

We can therefore decide to consolidate our unspent outputs into a single spendable output with the least possible waste of satoshi for transaction fees as we saw in Appendix I.

Consolidating the funds on your light wallet is quite simple: just copy a reception address and send the maximum amount to it, always remembering to first establish the fees you wish to pay.

Glossary

Some of the most common terms in the industry.

Bear market: definition used to describe the periods in which the market is falling. Usually these are extended periods of time, typically months.

Blockstream Satellite network: a network of satellites created by the Blockstream company in order to send valid Bitcoin blocks to Earth. The aim is to offer Bitcoin a mesh network for its proper functioning, without using the Internet.

Broadcast system: Bitcoin, in its base layer meaning, is often referred to as a broadcast system because, although transactions travel without the direct intervention of a reliable third party, miners are in charge of transcribing them into the blockchain. However, it is not possible to censor transactions because, if a miner did not include them in a block, they would still be included by someone else in a subsequent block.

Bug: error in writing software that can cause systemic malfunctions or crashes.

Capital control: measures taken by central authorities to regulate the flow of money into and out of the state economy.

Change: the rest of a Bitcoin transaction. Bitcoin uses the UTXO model, so each transaction corresponds to a certain number of unspent bitcoins (outputs) used as input to the latter.
Let's imagine that Alice has to send 1 BTC to Bob and her wallet has 1.25 BTC as unspent bitcoins (output). Alice will send Bob the entire output of 1.25 BTC, pay a variable mining commission (for example 0.0001 BTC) and Bob will hold 1 BTC. Alice will then receive 0.2499 BTC as the transaction change, usable for the next expenses.

Circulating supply: the amount of bitcoins in circulation at this time. All the bitcoins generated up to this point are considered, although the actual circulating supply should consider bitcoins whose keys have not been lost and which are therefore expendable.

CoinJoin: system used to increase the fungibility of Bitcoin transactions on blockchain. CoinJoin combines multiple payments from different senders in a single transaction.

Cold Wallet: typically offline wallet, on which most of our wealth in satoshi should be preserved.

Deflation: economic phenomenon opposed to inflation. Decrease in the price of goods or services for an extended period of time. Causes the increase in the purchasing power of the currency.

Difficulty adjustment: A miner closes a block on average every 10 minutes. The calculation of the Proof of Work involves a variable difficulty which means that the average time of discovery of the blocks is precisely 10 minutes. This difficulty is adjusted every 2016 blocks, about two weeks. If, in this interval of time, the hashrate of the miners has increased to the point of reducing the time of discovery of the blocks to less than 10 minutes, then the difficulty will increase, if instead the average time is greater than 10 minutes it will be reduced.

Fiat: legal currencies, with a forced market, in which the rule of inconvertibility between banknotes and any precious metals held by the State applies. An example of fiat money is given by the Dollar, the Euro and the Pound. Almost all the classical currencies in circulation are fiat.

FOMO: literally Fear Of Missing Out, or fear of being cut off. Indicates the anxiety that is typically generated in periods in which the price of an asset, and therefore also bitcoin, increases rapidly. Many are drawn to buy from this sudden price increase, hoping to generate a profit just as quickly.

FUD: Fear, Uncertainty and Doubt, represent the dissemination of information, even false or otherwise manipulated in order to reduce the price of an asset or discourage its purchase.

Gold Standard: monetary system in which currencies are representations of a certain amount of gold and are convertible. Until 1971 the Dollar was "backed by gold", ie it represented a certain amount of gold stored in the Federal Reserve vaults.

Halving: division by two. In Bitcoin it indicates the halving of the subsidy to the miner who discovers a new block and takes place about every four years, that is after 210,000 blocks, starting from block 0 called Genesis Block. Currently (2019) the reward is 12.5 bitcoins and will become 6.25 BTC in 2020. Bitcoin inflation increases with this reduction.

Hash: non-invertible mathematical function. Thanks to it, it is possible to transform a string of data of arbitrary length into a string of predefined length.

Hierarchical Deterministic Wallet (HD Wallet): a wallet that generates new receiving addresses each time one is used to receive funds. This type of wallet allows you to control theoretically infinite addresses using a single main private key (Master Private Key). Hierarchical deterministic wallets are useful in increasing the privacy level of blockchain transactions.

HODL: neologism that indicates the action of saving bitcoins trying not to spend them. The user who acts in this way defines himself as a hodler.

Inflation: price inflation means increase in the price of goods or services over an extended period of time. Causes the decrease in the purchasing power of the currency. Monetary inflation means increase in the supply of a monetary system.

Master Private Key: main private key of a hierarchical deterministic wallet. Through the Master Private Key it is possible to derive all the past and future addresses of the wallet.

Mesh network: a decentralized connection system that uses nodes that act as receivers, transmitters and repeaters. A mesh network may not need to be connected to the Internet.

Seed phrase: a list of words (typically 12 or 24) randomly generated by our wallet. These words, put in sequence, allow the wallet to generate all the addresses linked to a specific Master Private Key.

Shitcoin: alternative cryptocurrencies are often referred to as altcoin or shitcoin. The decentralization and security features of Bitcoin are often reduced or eliminated in favor of the speed of blockchain transactions.

Smart contract: digital contracts regulated by protocols, which do not require direct human intervention for their execution.

Ticker: the symbol used to identify an asset in the market. Bitcoin ticker is BTC

Token: typically an asset that is hosted by another blockchain.
There are tokens whose mission is to be considered real cryptocurrencies, others are utilities. Some represent a project that in the future could have its own mainet (a proprietary blockchain) and will be exchanged with the assets of this mainet typically in a 1:1 ratio. Other tokens allow you to purchase the goods and/or services of the project in question. Finally, there are definable security tokens which, like the classic stock market, represent a participation in the project, in terms of dividends, profits, governance, etc.

Total supply: the total bitcoins that will be put into circulation. We know this quantity and we know in which block this will be reached, even if not the precise time. The predictability of Bitcoin is one of its fundamental characteristics.

Whales: a great market player. Typically, when a "whale" sells or buys large sums of money, the market suffers more or less markedly. In finance these players are sometimes identified with the term "shark", although by this definition we mean an actor who acts aggressively on the market even without having the capital of the so-called whales.

About the author

IT consultant, photographer, music lover, #Bitcoin enthusiast.

David Coen is an IT consultant and professional photographer with over 10 years of experience.

In 2016 David undertook the study of Bitcoin and is convinced that we are facing a technological revolution equal to the one that led to the adoption of the Internet and the World Wide Web.

He supports the adoption of the LNP/BP terminology to indicate the suite of protocols at the base of Bitcoin (Settlement Layer) and of the second layer Lightning Network (Transaction Layer).

Contacts

How can I help you?

Send a message to:
email: info@davidcoen.it
Twitter: @thedavidcoen
Website: davidcoen.it
PGP Fingerprint: 5351632CBBF23EF29F1815ACD270A7681AE508EA

Sources and References

[1] S. Nakamoto, Bitcoin: A Peer-to-Peer Electronic Cash System, 2008.

[2] C. Valia, "Le carte del circuito Visa hanno smesso di funzionare in tutta Europa e nel Regno Unito," The Post International, 1 June 2018. [Online]. Available: https://www.tpi.it/2018/06/01/visa-down/.

[3] The Guardian, "Visa card payments system returns to full capacity after crash," The Guardian, June 2018. [Online]. Available: https://www.theguardian.com/money/2018/jun/01/visa-card-network-crashes-and-sparks-payment-chaos.

[4] M. Arnold, "MasterCard customers suffer outages around the world," Financial Times, 12 July 2018. [Online]. Available: https://www.ft.com/content/1fd2a066-860f-11e8-a29d-73e3d454535d.

[5] J. Sternberg, "MasterCard's Server Went Down. And Twitter Users Raged Because They Couldn't Get Their Dunkin' Fix," Adweek, 10 May 2018. [Online]. Available: https://www.adweek.com/digital/mastercards-server-went-down-and-twitter-raged-because-it-couldnt-get-its-dunkin-fix/.

[6] B. Scott, "The Guardian," 19 July 2018. [Online]. Available: https://www.theguardian.com/commentisfree/2018/jul/19/cashless-society-con-big-finance-banks-closing-atms.

[7] U. G. HM Treasury. [Online]. Available: https://assets.publishing.service.gov.uk/government/uploads/system/uploads/attachment_data/file/689234/Cash_and_digital_payments_in_the_new_economy.pdf.

[8] N. Fabris, "Cashless Society – The Future of Money or a Utopia?," in Journal of Central Banking Theory and Practice, 2010, pp. 53-66.

[9] R. Huang, "How Bitcoin And WikiLeaks Saved Each Other," 26 April 2019. [Online]. Available: https://www.forbes.com/sites/rogerhuang/2019/04/26/how-bitcoin-and-wikileaks-saved-each-other/.

[10] J. Andrews and J. Rampen, "Greece crisis: Banks closed and cash machines limited to €60 a day - what you can do," [Online]. Available: https://www.mirror.co.uk/money/greek-crisis-travel-advice-cash-machines-limited-banks-closed-5967293.

[11] P. Sanders, "Argentina Imposes Capital Controls as Reserves Drain Away," 1 September 2019. [Online]. Available: https://www.bloomberg.com/news/articles/2019-09-01/argentina-imposes-currency-controls-as-debt-crisis-escalates.

[12] Il Post, "La crisi di Hong Kong, spiegata bene," 17 August 2019. [Online]. Available: https://www.ilpost.it/2019/08/17/crisi-hong-kong-spiegata/.

[13] P. Siu, "Hong Kong slow to go cashless? Blame success of Octopus card, minister says," 30 October 2017. [Online]. Available: https://www.scmp.com/news/hong-kong/economy/article/2117467/hong-kong-slow-go-cashless-blame-success-octopus-card.

[14] M. Hui, "Why Hong Kong's protesters were afraid to use their metro cards," 13 June 2019. [Online]. Available: https://qz.com/1642441/extradition-law-why-hong-kong-protesters-didnt-use-own-metro-cards/.

[15] A. Vranova, T. Ajiboye, L. Buenaventura, L. Liu, A. Lloyd, A. Machado, J. Song and A. Gladstein, The Little Bitcoin Book: Why Bitcoin Matters for Your Freedom, Finances, and Future, 2019.

[16] H. R. Foundation, "Political Regime Map," [Online]. Available: https://hrf.org/research_posts/political-regime-map/.

[17] V. Marria, "Forbes," 21 December 2018. [Online]. Available: https://www.forbes.com/sites/vishalmarria/2018/12/21/what-a-cashless-society-could-mean-for-the-future/.

[18] Crypto Italia, "Why is the limit 21 million BTC?," [Online]. Available: https://cryptoitalia.org/en/why-is-the-limit-21-million-btc/.

[19] Floyd, David, "17 Millionth Bitcoin Was Mined: What Does It Mean And Why Does This Matter?," 27 April 2018. [Online]. Available: https://www.coindesk.com/17-millionth-bitcoin-mined-means-matters

[20] J. Song, "Understanding Segwit Block Size," 3 July 2017. [Online]. Available: https://medium.com/@jimmysong/understanding-segwit-block-size-fd901b87c9d4.

[21] J. Song, "Transaction Malleability Explained," 16 August 2017. [Online]. Available: https://bitcointechtalk.com/transaction-malleability-explained-b7e240236fc7.

[22] J. Lopp, "Who Controls Bitcoin Core?," [Online]. Available: https://blog.lopp.net/who-controls-bitcoin-core-/.

[23] Fidest, "oundreef viene riconosciuta ufficialmente dall'Intellectual Property Office del Regno Unito come Independent Management Entity (IME)," 2016. [Online]. Available: https://fidest.wordpress.com/2016/04/04/soundreef-viene-riconosciuta-ufficialmente-dallintellectual-property-office-del-regno-unito-come-independent-management-entity-ime/.

[24] Blockchain.com, "Average Number Of Transactions Per Block," [Online]. Available: https://www.blockchain.com/charts/n-transactions-per-block.

[25] R. A. Werner, "How do banks create money, and why can other firms not do the same? An explanation for the coexistence of lending and deposit-taking," in International Review of Financial Analysis, Vol. 36, 2014, pp. 71-77.

[26] F. C. A. (FCA), "Client money rules," [Online]. Available: https://www.handbook.fca.org.uk/handbook/CASS/7.pdf.

[27] "Laszlo's Pizza," [Online]. Available: https://bitcointalk.org/index.php?topic=137.0.

[28] "Laszlo's Pizza Transaction," [Online]. Available: https://blockchair.com/bitcoin/transaction/a1075db55d416d3ca199f55b6084e2115b9345e16c5cf302fc80e9d5fbf5d48d.

[29] Investopedia, "Money Supply," [Online]. Available: https://www.investopedia.com/terms/m/moneysupply.asp.

[30] M. Hartman, "Here's how much money there is in the world — and why you've never heard the exact number," Business Insider, 17 November 2017. [Online]. Available: https://www.businessinsider.com/heres-how-much-money-there-is-in-the-world-2017-10?IR=T.

[31] P. Hobson, "Exclusive: Fake-branded bars slip dirty gold into world markets," Reuters, 28 August 2019. [Online]. Available: https://www.reuters.com/article/us-gold-swiss-fakes-exclusive/exclusive-fake-branded-bars-slip-dirty-gold-into-world-markets-idUSKCN1VI0DD.

[32] B. Musser, "What is the Lightning Network?," Airbitz Inc., 28 March 2019. [Online]. Available: https://edge.app/blog/what-is-the-lightning-network/.

[33] L. Law, S. Sabett and J. Solinas, "HOW TO MAKE A MINT: THE CRYPTOGRAPHY OF ANONYMOUS ELECTRONIC CASH," National Security Agency Office of Information Security Research and Technology, 1996. [Online]. Available: https://groups.csail.mit.edu/mac/classes/6.805/articles/money/nsamint/nsamint.htm.

[34] StackExchange, "Badr Bellaj about Bitcoin private key security," [Online]. Available: https://bitcoin.stackexchange.com/questions/2847/how-long-would-it-take-a-large-computer-to-crack-a-private-key#targetText=A%20Bitcoin%20private%20key%20(ECC,universe%20to%20count%20them%20all.

[35] B. Musser, "Hardware, Software, and Programmable Security," Airbitz Inc., [Online]. Available: https://edge.app/blog/hardware-software-and-programmable-security/.

[36] V. Buterin, "On Bitcoin Maximalism, and Currency and Platform Network Effects," 19 November 2014. [Online]. Available: https://blog.ethereum.org/2014/11/20/bitcoin-maximalism-currency-platform-network-effects/.

[37] V. G. Cerf and R. E. Kahn, "A Protocol for Packet Network Intercommunication," Princeton University, 1974. [Online]. Available: https://www.cs.princeton.edu/courses/archive/fall06/cos561/papers/cerf74.pdf.

[38] V. Yadav, "Learning the TCP/IP Protocol Suite," 11 March 2018. [Online]. Available: https://codeburst.io/learning-tcp-ip-protocol-suite-6947b601ea11.

[39] "Internet protocol suite," Wikipedia, [Online]. Available: https://en.wikipedia.org/wiki/Internet_protocol_suite.

[40] A. Ol, "Internet Protocol stack in Internet protocol suite (TCP/IP)," 18 OCtober 2017. [Online]. Available: https://medium.com/@anna7/internet-protocol-layers-in-internet-protocol-suite-tcp-ip-abe038c0adde.

[41] T. D. Joseph Poon, "The Bitcoin Lightning Network: Scalable Off-Chain Instant Payments," 14 January 2016. [Online]. Available: https://lightning.network/lightning-network-paper.pdf.

[42] T. Dryja, "Discreet Log Contracts," MIT Digital Currency Initiative, [Online]. Available: https://adiabat.github.io/dlc.pdf.

[43] "Storm on GitHub," [Online]. Available: https://github.com/storm-org/storm-spec.

[44] A. v. Wirdum, "With Stratum V2, Braiins Plans Big Overhaul in Pooled Bitcoin Mining," Bitcoin Magazine, 5 August 2019. [Online]. Available: https://bitcoinmagazine.com/articles/with-stratum-v2-braiins-plans-big-overhaul-in-pooled-bitcoin-mining.

[45] C. Reichel, "BetterHash Protocol Lets Pool Miners Regain Control Over Their Hash Power," Bitcoin Magazine, 21 January 2019. [Online]. Available: https://bitcoinmagazine.com/articles/betterhash-protocol-lets-pool-miners-regain-control-over-their-hash-power.

[46] Coin Dance, "Bitcoin Nodes Summary," [Online]. Available: https://coin.dance/nodes.

www.ingramcontent.com/pod-product-compliance
Lightning Source LLC
Chambersburg PA
CBHW070624220526
45466CB00001B/92